# Aid Effectiveness in Africa

## Developing Trust between Donors and Governments

PHYLLIS R. POMERANTZ

LEXINGTON BOOKS
*Lanham • Boulder • New York • Toronto • Oxford*

LEXINGTON BOOKS

Published in the United States of America
by Lexington Books
An imprint of The Rowman & Littlefield Publishing Group, Inc.
4501 Forbes Boulevard, Suite 200, Lanham, Maryland 20706

PO Box 317
Oxford
OX2 9RU, UK

British Library Cataloguing in Publication Information Available

**Library of Congress Cataloging-in-Publication Data**

Pomerantz, Phyllis R., 1953–
   Aid effectiveness in Africa : developing trust between donors and governments /
Phyllis R. Pomerantz.
      p. cm.
   Includes bibliographical references and index.
   ISBN 0-7391-1002-0 (cloth : alk. paper) — ISBN 0-7391-1003-9 (pbk. : alk. paper)
   1. Economic assistance—Africa. 2. Economic development—Social aspects—
Africa. 3. Trust. 4. Interorganizational relations—Africa. 5. Africa—Foreign economic
relations. I. Title.

   HC800.P657 2004
   338.91'096—dc22                                                           2004015933

Printed in the United States of America

∞™ The paper used in this publication meets the minimum requirements of American
National Standard for Information Sciences—Permanence of Paper for Printed Library
Materials, ANSI/NISO Z39.48-1992.

# Contents

# Preface

This is not the book I set out to write. I planned to write a semi-scholarly book on aid with case studies from the two countries in Africa I knew best—Mozambique and Zambia. But as often happens, the book took on a life of its own. I was on a sabbatical from the World Bank when I wrote most of it. As I got further away from the ups and downs of everyday life as a country director for the Bank, I realized that I wanted to try and reach a larger audience and not write a book just for my colleagues in the "industry." What follows is definitely not a standard treatise on aid effectiveness—there are no tables or graphs. And there's almost no mention of money—even though I hasten to add that I think the money is important.

But money alone will not bring sustained development to Africa. Neither donor-driven aid nor countries "going it alone" has led to widespread success on the development front. So there has to be a third way: one that blends Africa's reality—its history, its politics and society, and its culture—with the best lessons of international experience. A true blending requires a true partnership. So this is a book about relationships, and about how trust can lead to mutual influence and lasting change. Viewed from that prism, it is hard not to develop a critical perspective on aid in Africa today. If we, the donors, are to develop trust and trusting relationships with our African colleagues, it will mean a fundamental change in the way we work. Are we prepared to do that? More importantly, are our countries' legislatures, nongovernmental organizations, and the public at large poised for a change in the foreign aid industry?

While aid budgets may increase or decrease, little real change will happen without a more broadly shared understanding of the dilemmas of aid and development in Africa. So I decided to take advantage of my personal and professional experiences—and to rely on the wisdom of colleagues and friends. I returned to Africa in September 2000 to interview senior aid representatives and government officials in Mozambique and Zambia. I also interviewed a number of country directors for the World Bank in Africa. Every quote I have used is verbatim, but I have maintained strict confidentiality other than identifying the voice as either that of a donor or that of a government official. It was the only way to get people to talk candidly and openly.

Many—especially those who had known me in my official capacity—were perhaps surprised at the interest that a hard-driving World Bank official was showing in the "soft side of aid." All I can say is that I increasingly believe that this is not the soft side, but the solid core of successful development efforts. I am sure that others who read this book will wonder why I have not tried to balance the story out, focusing on the shortcomings of the governments as well as those of the donors. I have left that half of the equation to those more qualified—the African governments and the people they serve. And finally, there are those who will speculate on why I have chosen a fairly critical perspective and will worry that I "am biting the hand that feeds me." But those who truly know the "aid scene" today in most of Africa, those who are engaged in the many efforts to reform aid relationships, those who believe in the World Bank's mission ("Our dream is a world free of poverty"), and those who are determined to lead their citizens to a better life on the African continent will understand. I am not one of the disgruntled, low-morale aid officials I talk about in the book. Quite the contrary: Despite the difficulties ahead—and with greater public understanding and support—I believe that we can and will make changes. I wanted to contribute.

Needless to say, the views expressed herein are my personal ones and in no way represent the official views of the World Bank. I have many people to thank: Callisto Madavo, Jean Louis Sarbib, Richard Stern, Praful Patel, and Katherine Sierra, all of whom made the writing (and rewriting) of this book possible; Alan Gelb, Ian Goldin, Terry Barnett, and Farida Pomerantz for helpful comments on earlier drafts; Carol Lancaster for giving me some early pointers; Michael Fairbanks, for giving me my first window on the culture and development debate; the staff of the World Bank's Mozambique and Zambia offices for invaluable logistical assistance; my colleagues, current and former country directors for the World Bank, who gave me both encouragement and materials I used in this book; Seth Beckerman for careful editing of an early version of the manuscript; Valentina Kalk and Arianne Wessal of the World Bank and Serena Krombach, Brian Richards, and their colleagues at Lexington Books for invaluable assistance in the book's publication; and students at UNC, Duke, and Georgetown who have listened and commented upon presentations I've made based on the manuscript. I need to acknowledge the vast list of colleagues—World Bank staff and consultants, colleagues from donor agencies resident throughout the world, colleagues from nongovernmental organizations, and colleagues throughout Mozambique and Zambia—who are present, in one form or another, in this book. A very special acknowledgment and thank you go to the ambassadors and other aid officials in Zambia and Mozambique who kindly consented to be interviewed for this book, and most especially to the senior government officials who not only took the time to speak with me, but told me I needed to write this book.

The endnotes and references at the end of this book do not do justice to the intellectual dialog I have had through time with many of the authors, even with the ones I have yet to meet. I thank them all for providing me with intellectual stimulation and good debates. And finally, I am grateful to Charles, C. and D.—who remind me that life is always full of surprises and everyday pleasures.

# 1

# Foreign Aid Is Not Just Money

This is a book about foreign aid in Africa, but it's not about money. It is about relationships, and especially about trust—how to create it, how to use it, and perhaps most importantly, how not to lose or abuse it. This is not to say that money is not important. The money—foreign aid—is critically important, but money alone hasn't been enough to change the lives of most poor Africans. Nearly 1 trillion dollars of foreign aid has gone to Africa over the last half-century, but poverty has increased. Average per capita income is now lower than at the end of the 1960s.[1]

Part of the problem is that there is no "magic bullet" or set formula to end poverty in Africa (or anywhere else, for that matter). When I first started working in Africa, I was struck that my previously unquestioned Western notion of unilinear progress no longer applied. Just because you build a road doesn't mean there will still be a road in the same place ten years from now. The reasons why are complex—the natural problem of fast-growing vegetation, not to mention floods and other disasters; skill issues affecting design, construction, and maintenance standards; corruption that taints materials and quality; shifting population and hence road use patterns; lack of community awareness and involvement; and the perennial budget deficits of African governments squeezing out, if not totally eliminating, money for road maintenance. Sometimes it's just one of these factors that makes the road disappear; sometimes it's all of them. And sometimes, it's hard to tell precisely what the problem is.

The absence of a magic bullet means that a lot of money—both from Africans and from abroad—gets wasted. Some, undeniably, gets wasted on the headline grabbers: civil wars or wars with neighbors; high-level corruption and outright stealing; and shiny monuments. But probably far more gets wasted with the best of intentions—on development programs that simply don't work or don't endure.

Sometimes, however, when you return the road is still there or even improved. There *are* many successful foreign aid and development programs. Each time a new school is opened—or for that matter, when inflation drops from 70 percent a year to 0 (as it did in Mozambique in the mid-1990s)—people's lives are not only changed but changed for the better. There has even been success with major epidemics: thanks to a successful partnership between governments and foreign donors, river blindness, responsible for robbing millions of Africans of their sight, may be virtually eliminated in our lifetime.[2] The trick is figuring out what has been successful and why, and how to make it last—in other words, "how to get the most bang out of a buck."

## AID EFFECTIVENESS

There is a pressing need for more sustainable results and poverty reduction in Africa—what we in the aid business refer to as "aid effectiveness." The need for aid effectiveness, coupled with spotty success thus far, has spawned impatience and anxiety, which in turn have given rise to a number of "aid neuroses." These are easily recognizable to those of us who work in the business. There are obsessive disorders, for example, "aid fads" and "aid darlings." Examples of aid fads that swept the development landscape at one time or another, and that mostly didn't work, include integrated rural development (area-based, multiactivity projects combining social and economic activities and infrastructure in a single project), the basic needs approach (concentrating on basic social services for the poorest), and development banking projects (jumpstarting local businesses by making credit readily available, frequently with some sort of subsidy). Once the fad ends, there seems to be no one who remembers why we thought it was a good idea in the first place—that is, until the fad reemerges twenty or thirty years later in a repackaged form with a different name.

Obsession also occurs with individual countries. Kenya, Ghana, Zambia, and Zimbabwe at one time have all been "aid darlings"—countries that donors single out and provide massive support to based on an optimistic view that they could "make it" and provide the positive role model the rest of Africa needs. Today's aid darlings are Mozambique, Uganda, and Tanzania. The trouble with aid darlings is that they seldom last. Maybe Mozambique and Uganda will prove to be the exception to this rule; both have sustained economic growth and donor goodwill for over a decade. But neither is out of the woods: Mozambique is facing an important political transition when President Joaquim Chissano steps down, and Uganda continues to be plagued by rebels in part of the country. Both, at least at this juncture, can hardly be described as stable democracies. And Tanzania regularly falls in and out of fashion: this is the third or fourth time it has achieved "darling" status.

And that brings us to aid "mood-swings." Yesterday's darlings can become today's "failed states," leading to a dramatic drop in donor support. Undeniably, this happens in most cases because of real and substantive policy differences between the African government in question and the international aid community, for example, Zimbabwean President Mugabe's widely publicized failure to curb rural violence related to the seizure of white-owned farms by blacks and to hold free and fair elections. But beyond the objective facts are very real feelings of disappointment, failed expectations, and even betrayal among the donor representatives. Perspectives can and do become warped. Similar to what happens with individuals who suffer from manic depression, the "highs" are high, but the "lows" are really low.

## THE IMPERATIVE OF SUCCESS

Not surprisingly, the foreign aid industry is hypercritical of itself and has created a whole subindustry of evaluation and critique. Freud might have said that we have an unrelenting collective superego. The World Bank has an independent Operations Evaluation Department dedicated to reviewing and critiquing World Bank operations and programs. Many individual donor countries have sponsored major reviews of aid programs, their own and others. Multidonor groups, such as the Special Program for Africa (SPA), debate how to improve aid effectiveness. The literature on foreign aid and its effectiveness is massive—there are individual project evaluations, country reviews, subregional reviews, regional reviews on specific topics, and a world of articles and books written by scholars and practitioners. The aid culture is so prone to self-criticism that the late 1990s saw a concerted effort by the World

Bank and others to identify "lessons of success." This has led to a resurgence of the debates that took place in the early 1970s on designing monitoring and evaluation systems. Why? Because it's not so easy to measure success when there is a big time lag between the initial investment and the payoff. How can I be sure that the dollar I spend today on building a school will really increase a child's earning capacity ten years from now?

The need to measure success and show results is not only because solving, or even mitigating, the continent's desperate poverty is urgent. It is directly related to the syndrome of "aid fatigue." Beginning in the early 1990s, aid budgets began falling.[3] The difficulties in getting aid appropriations through the U.S. Congress have been well publicized, and the United States was not alone. Up until September 11, 2001, and the attack on the World Trade Center, aid budgets in all major donor countries were having a hard time. Since then, there appears to be increased recognition that development and peace are mutually reinforcing.[4] The European Union, the United States, and Canada have all announced aid increases.

It remains to be seen whether increases in aid will be sustained over the decade or whether they represent a temporary reaction to the events of September 11. It also remains to be seen how much of the aid increases will be directed toward Sub-Saharan Africa. The year 2003 witnessed another dramatic shift as reconstruction in Iraq—and its price tag—monopolized the attention of some key donors.[5] This is not the first time that Africa has moved to the "back burner." The drop in aid during the 1990s reflected Africa's perceived lack of strategic importance in the post–Cold War era. It seemed that globalization was leaving Africa behind—or at least in the slow lane.[6] As Thomas Friedman said in *The Lexus and the Olive Tree*, there is no more First World and Third World, just the Fast World and the Slow World.[7]

In some countries, the drop in aid in the 1990s reflected domestic politics, internal pressures, or regional interests closer to home. But African aid fatigue is also clearly linked to the feeling that not much has been accomplished with the money spent. Aid fatigue used to be a malady of some portion of the public and of legislators worldwide, but skepticism has further increased among these groups. What is truly striking today is that aid fatigue is increasingly articulated by people in the business itself—diplomats, international officials, and development workers.[8] And while September 11 may have loosened the purse strings slightly, the skepticism has not abated. The United States has made it clear that more aid will only go to countries who are willing to adopt sound policies and who are able to show results. "Results-based aid" and "performance metrics" are the new buzzwords in the development community.

Impatience for results, aid fatigue, and what some have called "Afro-pessimism" are related to the "big picture" and expectations. In the 1990s, the demise of apartheid, the advent of Western-style multiparty democracies (or at least elections) in a number of countries, and the presence of several so-called enlightened African leaders seemed to usher in a new era. There was talk of an African Renaissance, a term first used by then Deputy President Thabo Mbeki of South Africa. The Renaissance was short-lived. The last part of that decade saw fighting in many parts of the continent, natural disasters in Southern Africa, and an exponential growth in HIV/AIDS throughout the continent. By early 2000, Africa was once again being dubbed "the hopeless continent."[9] As the decade unfolds, African leaders are trying to revive the "Renaissance—and with it the optimism—through an initiative called the New Partnership for Africa's Development (NEPAD). There has been some success: peace efforts seem to be yielding results in a number of countries. But the fragility of peace in many areas, the economic and political "meltdown" in Zimbabwe, and the spread of HIV/AIDS continue to cast a pall.

There is a danger, then, that aid fatigue will settle in for good if we are unable to sustain good news about Africa and show results. I use "we" in this context not because I believe that non-Africans are responsible for or can ultimately determine what happens on that continent. Foreign aid is, however, an integral part of Africa's past and an essential part of its future. So it's not surprising that there is lively debate on how best to divvy up what is, in any event, inadequate to begin with.[10]

## CRITERIA FOR AID

What are the criteria for selecting who gets aid and how much? There are understandably many different answers to that question. For some countries such as the United States, strategic and security-related concerns are a big factor. The United States in 2000 doubled its spending on HIV/AIDS, particularly in Africa. Shortly afterward, then President Clinton declared that the spread of AIDS was a strategic threat to the United States.[11] After the attack on the World Trade Center, security-related concerns provided one of the strongest rationales for U.S. aid: "When governments fail to meet the most basic needs of their people, these failed states can become havens for terror."[12] And now, following the war in Iraq, the U.S., of course, is engaged in a major aid and reconstruction effort.

For other countries (Canada and Japan are just two examples), home country business interests play a role in deciding who gets what and how much. Although weakening over time, history—colonial ties—is another selection criterion, particularly influential in British, French, and Portuguese aid decisions. There are also somewhat more altruistic selection criteria. Need is one of them. There is a renewed, explicit focus on poverty reduction by some development agencies (most notably, the World Bank and the British Department for International Development [DFID]). Humanitarian concerns have also traditionally been important in the Nordic countries. It makes intuitive sense to put the aid where it is needed most by the most people, yet need-based criteria immediately bump against the reality of performance. In countries where there is massive civil strife or war (e.g., Sudan) or a dysfunctional government (e.g., Zaire under Mobutu, Zimbabwe under Mugabe), development aid, despite the desperate need, is ineffective.

The extreme cases are easy to identify, but after the extremes, identification becomes more difficult. Less dramatic performance-based criteria have been at the center of the debate. A number of recent studies have argued that countries with good economic policies and institutions absorb more aid more effectively.[13] Simply put, there's a clear message—aid will be most effective when it rewards the good performers. Who are the good performers? They are the ones who are willing and able to carry out fundamental economic and social reforms.

What's the problem with allocating aid based on performance? Well, first of all, the jury is still out on whether the research that supports performance-based aid decisions is sufficiently robust. Subsequent studies have both supported and called into question whether there is, in fact, a positive connection between good policies and effective aid.[14] But even if the research is correct, "picking winners" based on performance is a tricky business. First of all, good performers are not necessarily those that are strategically important or where businesses from donor countries have traditionally invested. Some donors are reluctant to give up parochial interests in their aid decisions. The second problem is that good performance and poverty often don't go hand-in-hand. For donors with humanitarian motivations, it is difficult or even illogical to walk away from the poor because a particular government is unwilling or unable to carry out reforms.

There are even more troubling issues. What does it mean to be a good performer? In academic research, you can construct a definition. But when you are a decision-maker and events are happening in "real time," it can be exceedingly difficult to tell the difference between an emerging winner (for example, Mozambique in 1992) and an emerging disappointment (Angola in 1996). This is not only the case with countries coming out of conflict. Even in countries free of conflict, promising economic reform programs have faltered and failed. While events are swirling around you, it is hard to tell the difference between a temporary setback and the start of a fundamental change in direction. Most reform programs are fragile, not the least because by definition, they are taking place in less than ideal circumstances *and* attacking vested interests.

What exactly constitutes good policy and good reforms? On the economic front, there may be some convergence, at least among the donor countries, on the principles of market-based economies, but the specific reforms, and their sequencing and timing, are frequently debatable. Needless to say, even the enthusiasm about market-based principles is hardly universal. Moreover, for some donors, political criteria related to "good government"—political governance—have become just as important, if not more important, in assessing performance than strictly economic criteria. And strictly economic criteria have been expanded to include judgments on institutional performance and economic governance criteria, such as efforts to combat corruption. Different donors have different criteria, and it is not uncommon for the international community to disagree about just how favorable the policy environment is.

In reality, there are few clear-cut situations in Africa today and no "perfect reformers." With the exception of the war-torn societies, most countries in Africa today are "uncertain reformers." Why uncertain? Because we don't know if reform will continue and if the reforms will actually yield the expected benefits. No wonder, even with a seemingly clear signpost of "performance," it is so difficult to make aid decisions and for the public to make sense of aid decisions.

But decisions do have to be made. Too often in the past each donor has made decisions independently—without much consultation with other donors or even with the recipient government. The result in many countries has been an "aid bazaar": lots of good ideas, lots of projects, and lots of wasted money. In many countries, it has been fairly common to find overlapping and competing projects and, at the same time, critical areas of neglect. The donors are well aware of this. Over the last thirty-five years, there have been continuing calls to improve aid coordination and harmonize the criteria and performance standards that donors apply in each country. And in the last few years, there has been some progress. To help reconcile performance and needs, donors now insist that governments receiving assistance have a clear written strategy to reduce poverty (PRSP or Poverty Reduction Strategy Paper). Also, in some countries, there is a new effort to place all donor assistance within a mutually agreed—among the government, civil society, and donors—comprehensive long-term development strategy (CDF or Comprehensive Development Framework).[15]

How much progress is being made on the aid coordination and harmonization front is an open question, one we will return to later, especially in chapter 6. Money is a crucial part of the story, but it's not the whole story. The same studies that found that aid is used most effectively in good policy environments also found that there is little evidence that aid has had a positive effect in uncertain or hostile policy environments.[16] Just like "money can't buy you love," money apparently also can't buy you reform.

## MORE THAN MONEY

So there's more to aid that just money. There are nonfinancial aspects to aid—policy advice and technical assistance, as well as the policy conditions and timing decisions that go along with the money. In reality, there is a rich and often complex and dynamic relationship between donors and governments and among the donors in each country. *The quality of the relationship may, in fact, be more important in influencing policy directions and ensuring successful outcomes, than the money itself.*

That's what this book is about—the relationships. Before setting the stage for the following chapters, there are a few points that need to be underlined. First, by talking about relationships and influence, I don't mean to imply that influence or learning is in only one direction. In a good relationship, all parties change and adapt. You frequently hear good teachers say that they have learned as much or more from their students than vice versa. In Africa, despite what you might expect, it isn't always clear who is the teacher and who is the student. In any event, there's plenty of learning that needs to go on by all concerned.

The second point is that by concentrating on donors and writing about relationships and influence, I am not trying to shift the primary or even major responsibility for what takes place to the donors. It is up to each African country to determine the path it takes and to assume responsibility for the consequences—both good and bad. The colonial legacy and postindependence era of the past as well as the current breathtaking pace of globalization may be limiting, but nonetheless there are still choices. These must be made by the countries and not by donors.

Finally, in many African countries, civil society is playing an increasing role in national affairs. And in the donor countries, civil society already is an integral part of the policymaking process. The increasing importance of civil society in foreign aid and development decisions is a substantial topic in and of itself, but one that largely lies beyond the scope of this book. In what follows, civil society is discussed only in the narrow context of how its actions can affect the relationship between donors and African governments. The limited role of civil society is this book is neither social commentary nor a reflection of reality. Civil society is increasingly a central force in African development.

So why write about the donors if they are not at the center of this story? We need to go back to the concept of "uncertain reformers." The uncertainty means that things could go either way. Under one scenario, a country's policies, the aid it receives, and the outcomes it achieves begin to mutually support one another. This creates a nurturing environment for continuing reform and a *virtuous circle* of growth and poverty reduction. Under another scenario, a country falls back into a *vicious cycle* of failed reforms, ineffective aid, and continuing economic stagnation and poverty. Under these uncertain conditions—where a country could go either way—actions at the margin can make an appreciable difference.[17] Money, or at least money alone, cannot bring about big changes and is not particularly effective in these uncertain circumstances. So that brings us to the nonfinancial aspects of aid and the interplay between them and the decisions related to money—decisions about conditions, sequencing of actions, and timing. The starting point for this book is that under certain circumstances donor actions and their relationship with a country, and particularly with its government, can have a positive influence and help to shore up and sustain reforms. Conversely, donors can play a role in destabilizing and seriously undermining ongoing, but fragile, reform programs.

Why then hasn't there been more focus on the "soft side of aid"? There has been some, but it has mainly focused on the type of policy conditions attached to financial support, and more recently on the meaning and mechanics of partnership in the context of improved aid coordination.[18] There hasn't been more work on the "soft side" in part because the money has naturally stolen center stage. Much that is written about foreign aid centers around the substance of reform and the criteria for providing financial support and determining the amounts—in others words, the *what* and *how much*. This concentration is part of the explanation for the relative lack of attention to *how* aid agencies do their work and to their relationships with the countries.

Much more of the reluctance to write and think about aid relationships is that it makes people in the business nervous.[19] That's because it deals with messy stuff—behaviors, cultural norms, skills, motivations, and judgment calls. The economists who still make up the hard-core of the profession would rather stick to precise and relatively simple formulas—if you can get the incentives right, the right things will happen. This, of course, is an exaggeration. Many economists recognize that the relationship and the dialog are important, but they don't feel particularly qualified to deal with these issues on anything other than an ad hoc basis. Thus, they continue to concentrate on the *what* and *how much,* and get frustrated when their good (and sometimes not so good) advice is ignored.

Even writing about this topic opens one to criticism from both the right and the left. For the conservative, isolationist right, particularly in the United States, foreign aid to Africa, given either bilaterally or through multilateral development agencies such as the World Bank, is a waste of money and effort. There should be no money and no relationship. There may be some who think that a relationship in lieu of money is the way to go—it may still be a waste of effort, but it's cheaper. It bears repeating that money is an essential part of the foreign aid package. By focusing on the relationships, I am not making an argument for slashing aid budgets or providing alternatives. Money matters—it just can't work wonders by itself.[20]

Another group, a portion of what I would call the "dogmatic left," also thinks looking at the relationship is a waste of time. Why bother, they would argue, when one side has all the power and the money? All the aid agencies do is to push the governments around. The governments do what they are told, and all that happens is the poor get poorer. Why would the donors want to change their behavior and way of doing business? The status quo suits them. The relationship is one of dominance and subservience, end of story.

Not quite. For one thing, power and influence are not the same thing. Sometimes money or power can make people do what they don't want to do, but as soon as they can, they usually go back to doing what they want. Influence is much more subtle and lasting. Influence works by convincing others that what you think they should do is actually the right thing to do. There's no coercion and a greater chance for lasting change. You can always argue that donors are not interested in lasting change and that the status quo suits them fine. Even if you don't believe that donors have a genuine commitment to meaningful change and poverty reduction in Africa, in today's fast changing and troubled world, there is no such thing as the status quo. Change is not an option; it's a fact. And influence seems to be a more effective instrument of change than the exercise of raw power—and that brings us back to looking at the relationships.

Despite the queasiness of traditional economists—and the hostility of the right and the disbelief of the left—there are those who are genuinely interested in this topic. Senior officials from both donor agencies and African governments are convinced that we need to take a fresh and frank look at the ways we interact with each other. When I told an African head of state that I was writing about relationships between donors and governments and the ways in which donors could positively or negatively influence reform efforts, his quick reply was that he would like to be among the first to read this book.

## EXPLORING THE RELATIONSHIP
This book is an exploration of current realities and attitudes in the aid relationship, searching for lessons on how one goes about building a constructive relationship that leads to mutual influence. It refers to social science theory garnered from a variety of disciplines—anthropology, linguistics, sociology, economics, political science, management theory, and psychology. It relies on and is informed by many little stories about foreign aid in Africa culled from interviews and personal experience. Because I experienced events in Mozambique and Zambia firsthand in the late 1990s and from the unique position of being the World Bank's country director and chair of the Consultative Group (the group that brings together all of a country's donors) for those countries, there are more and more detailed stories from those countries.

When you boil it down, all of the sources seem to point to *trust* as the fundamental ingredient in relationships that lead to mutual influence. Trust, in turn, is based on some extent of shared purpose, commitment, reliability, familiarity, transparency, and honest and open communication. But cultural differences, communication and language, personalities, and institutional incentives can all get in the way and complicate the picture.

At this point, some of you may be silently asking, "So what else is new?" The answer is simple: this isn't new. As the social scientists Charles Lindblom and David Cohen said over twenty years ago, "For social problem solving, . . . people will always depend heavily on ordinary knowledge."[21] All this book intends to do is to apply some pretty basic social science thinking to the business of foreign aid and development assistance. It attempts to systematically look at these issues and transport them from the venue of after-dinner conversations into the mainstream discussion of aid effectiveness. It also is an attempt to humanize the foreign aid and development discussion about Africa so that more of the public at large can understand the difficulties and rewards of helping Africans out of poverty. Our involvement and knowledge about Africa shouldn't only be about emergency interventions to stop famines and wars.

Some of you may also be saying, "Where's the beef?" to use the outdated expression from a fast food commercial in the United States over a decade ago. What does it matter if you have a good relationship and lots of influence if you don't have anything good to say? What about the substance? What about the quality of policy advice that donors give African governments? It would be easy to duck this and say that many others have concentrated on the substantive policy questions. But it turns out that many of the things that will improve the quality of the advice—things like local knowledge and an ability to dialog—are also the things that will improve the relationship. To quote Lindblom and Cohen again: "What often obscures our appreciation of interaction as a method of problem solving is that interaction often—perhaps typically—produces both outcome and implementation together."[22] In other words, better interaction or a better relationship is often inseparable from better policies and better implementation of those policies. You've heard this before—the end can't be separated from the means.

The organization of what follows is straightforward. The next chapter looks at influence and the concept and components of trust in the aid setting. The following chapter reports on related findings from interviews with donors and government officials conducted in two African countries. The findings are used to zero in on those issues that seem to present the greatest obstacles to establishing trust and a more constructive relationship. The next two chapters focus on the problems associated with differing cultural assumptions and the external and internal institutional factors that combine to limit donor effectiveness. The final chapter reviews lessons, provides some concrete suggestions to improve the aid relationship, and draws overall conclusions about the prospects for improving aid effectiveness in Africa.

Two final notes before we begin the discussion on influence and trust, one having to do with language and one having to do with emphasis. It is common today for development agencies to refer to themselves euphemistically or optimistically as "aid partners" or "development partners." The older term, "donors," seems to have a paternalistic air about it and has seemingly been deemed politically incorrect. And some of the agencies, like the World Bank and the International Monetary Fund (IMF), are technically not donors since they don't give money, but rather provide low-interest loans. While the sentiments behind the name change may be noble, I have never heard an African, other than in a formal speech, refer to the aid agencies as anything other than donors. Even though this book is primarily not about the money, we shouldn't lose sight of the fact that money is needed and in some cases desperately needed. I have chosen to continue to refer to the development agencies collectively—both bilaterals (representing individual countries) and multilaterals (such as the World Bank, IMF, African Development Bank, and United Nations Development Program)—as donors.

Finally, there is intentional imbalance in what follows. Although there are references to the behaviors, attitudes, and institutional constraints of governments, the primary focus is on examining those attitudes, norms, behaviors, and practices among the donor community that help shape the relationship between it and African governments. It is time for the donor community to take a long and hard look at the way it has been conducting its business. This is not to say that any change that is needed—or that whatever has been good or bad to date—is the donors' responsibility alone. As will become evident in the next chapter, the elements and behaviors that create trust have to be present in all the parties—it truly "takes two to tango."

## NOTES

1. World Bank 2000, p. 1, and World Bank 1998, p. 2. This trend is continuing in the new century. According to the latest United Nations Development Programme's annual Human Development Report, fifty-four countries are poorer now than they were in 1990, many of those in Africa (UNDP 2003). There are several notable exceptions among African countries, including Botswana, Mauritius, Mozambique, and Uganda.

2. To learn more about the successful campaign against river blindness or onchocerciasis, see World Bank 2001 and the World Bank's website on onchocerciasis, available at www.worldbank.org/gper.

3. Official development assistance peaked at 69 billion dollars (in 1995 prices) in 1991. See World Bank 1998, pp. 7–9.

4. See the United Nations 2002.

5. In the aftermath of Iraq, the United Nations issued an appeal for funds for twenty-one "forgotten disasters," seventeen of which were in Africa. See "Forgotten Disasters," *The Economist*, November 22–28, 2003, pp. 45–46.

6. See for example, Jim Hoagland, "Africa Abandoned," *The Washington Post*, May 11, 2000, p. A35.

7. Friedman 1999, p. 42.

8. Van de Walle (1999) concurs with this view. See especially pp. 338–39.

9. For recent examples of Afro-pessimism, see Rieff 1998 and Holman 2004. "The hopeless continent" was the cover of the *Economist*, May 13–19, 2000.

10. The United Nations, the World Bank, and others have estimated that aid would need to double from about 50 billion dollars to 100 billion dollars annually if the poverty reduction goals set by the United Nations for 2015—the Millennium Development Goals—are to be met. So far, donors have committed to increasing aid by 16 billion dollars a year by 2006.

11. "AIDS is Declared Threat to Security," *The Washington Post*, April 30, 2000, p. A1.

12. George W. Bush speech to the Inter-American Development Bank, March 14, 2002.

13. The most influential of these has probably been the World Bank's *Assessing Aid* report (1998), based on research by Burnside and Dollar. See especially the

chapter entitled "Money Matters—In A Good Policy Environment," pp. 28–46. Other studies include Van de Walle and Johnston 1996 and Tsikada 1998.

14. Arguing both sides of this debate has become a "cottage industry" in recent years. See Burnside and Dollar 1997 and Collier and Dollar 1998, among others, on one side, and Easterly, Levine, and Roodman 2003 and Ian Vasquez 2003, among others, on the other.

15. On PRSPs, see World Bank 2001(b) and IDA and IMF 2002. On CDFs, see Wolfensohn 1999 and World Bank 2003.

16. See Deverajan et al. 2001, World Bank 1998, and Tsikata 1998.

17. The 2000 bestseller by Malcolm Gladwell, *The Tipping Point—How Little Things Can Make a Big Difference*, makes precisely this point and attempts to explain how it happens. His thesis is that epidemics, fads, and other forms of mass learning happen because of a few people with special attributes that help develop and spread new ideas, techniques that make messages clear and memorable ("sticky"), and the overall context.

18. On conditionality, among others, see Collier 1997 and Killick 1997. On partnerships, see Picciotto 1998, World Bank 2001, and Abugre 1999.

19. A small body of literature is slowly emerging. A workshop held in September 2003 at the School of Oriental and African Studies, University of London, "Order and Disjuncture: The Organisation of Aid and Development," began exploring related themes within aid organizations. See, for example, Biggs, Messerschmidt, and Gurung 2003 and Eyben 2003, two of the workshop papers.

20. For a good overview of the benefits of aid, and some of the critiques, see John Cassidy, "Helping Hands," *The New Yorker*, March 18, 2002, pp. 60–65.

21. Lindblom and Cohen 1979, p. 12.

22. Lindblom and Cohen 1979, p. 25.

# 2

# Trust in the Aid Setting

At the Middle East peace summit at Camp David in 2000, a photo op showed the dance between Ehud Barak of Israel and Yasser Arafat of Palestine as each, with diplomatic courtesy, insisted that the other go through the door first. President Clinton solved the impasse by opening the second double door and urging them to go through together. This struck me as a perfect metaphor for relationships, and particularly aid relationships. When there isn't a reasonable level of trust, elaborate mechanisms must be found to move forward together—in this case, opening the second double door. Moving forward is particularly difficult when there are millions of eyes watching—and judging. And without trust, there's no guarantee that there won't be a dramatic reversal, as the events in the Middle East have tragically shown since that meeting. In contrast, when the relationship is good, the public is supportive and trust exists, it doesn't matter who goes through the door first. No one notices. When was the last time you saw an article or a picture about Tony Blair and George W. Bush fighting about who enters the room first?

How then can African governments and the donors move through the door together? A vast amount of literature assumes that if you hold the purse strings, you control the door and can make the other enter the room—first or last, depending on your pleasure. But the history of Africa over the last thirty-five years shows that it's not that simple. Despite severe aid dependency, many African governments have refused to go through the door—whether it's into a room stocked with goods from a competitive market economy or a room stocked with ballots from a multiparty democracy.

Why African governments have refused to enter—or have entered only to retreat hastily—is not so hard to understand. Some governments say that each donor has a favorite door, so it's hard to know which is the right one to enter. There is some truth to this, and we will return to the subject of aid coordination later. Mostly, African governments claim that it's not the right door for them, either because of their unique circumstances or because being in the room won't solve the abject poverty and misery around them. Some claim that "the people" in their societies won't allow it. Others simply resent being told where to go or rightly fear that being in the room will rob them of personal fortunes or the ability to exercise arbitrary power.

The question facing donors is how to change this situation. Some voices clearly advocate walking away, letting things deteriorate to a point where there will be absolutely no choice but to change. This is "power politics" in its most raw form. In extreme cases and for fairly limited periods of time, for example, in Zaire in the last years of Mobutu, this has been accepted as a viable option. But in most African countries, the situation is less clear-cut, and the sheer magnitude of human suffering—not to mention security and commercial concerns—argues against walking away. In this era of globalization, dropping out is not an option.

And if money alone won't change the situation, then the relationship and the ability to influence become paramount. The last three decades of African history attest to this, but it is also corroborated by comments from senior government officials, aid officials, and diplomats. When asked who is the most influential donor in a particular country, both government officials and donors generally point to a donor who is not the biggest donor in dollar terms.[1] Some point to the World Bank or IMF, usually not because of the size of their purse but because of their roles as "gatekeepers." Unless the World Bank and IMF back a country's economic program, the government in question is unlikely to receive substantial support from other donors. Leaving aside the special role of the World Bank and IMF, when asked why certain donors have more influence than others, the answers typically sound like this: "They understand our problems. . . . They talk to us without threatening us. . . . They are not always right, but we know that they are committed to our people. . . . They don't condescend, and they tell us what's on their mind. . . . They have earned the government's trust. . . . The Ambassador has been a friend and our advocate in his country. . . . They listen to us first."

Conversely, comments by government officials provide insight about why certain donors, including some with considerable sums of aid money at their disposal, exercise less influence: "They keep changing the conditions and raising the bar; you never know where you stand with them. . . . Their people are more interested in their nice houses and servants than in us. . . . They never leave the capital city. . . . We don't appreciate being lectured to. . . . They come with ready-made solutions; they think that whatever is good for Chile is good for us. . . . They establish very difficult deadlines and conditions; they overestimate our capacity and ignore our political processes. . . . They think that just because they send us a black ambassador we will do whatever they say."

## TRUST

Most of the comments center around the quality of the relationship and the presence or lack of trust. How can trust be developed? Before turning to that question, we need to briefly examine the concept of trust itself. In recent years, a whole body of literature has grown up around trust and the related concept of social capital. Francis Fukuyama has argued that trust is central to economic progress: "A nation's well being, as well as its ability to compete, is conditioned by a single, pervasive cultural characteristic: the level of trust inherent in the society."[2] Related to this, a number of sociologists and economists now view "social capital"—the ability of people to work together for common purposes in groups and organizations—as a key variable in economic development.[3] Fukuyama essentially argues that trust builds social capital and hence positively influences a community or nation's ability to prosper. According to this argument, the more economically advanced countries all share relatively higher levels of trust and social capital.

Whether or not you buy this argument in its entirety, it does seem that trust is an important "social glue" and that some societies or nations are more likely to trust than others. At the very least, they have different definitions of trust. For example, in the United States today, legal instruments form the basis for collaboration and trust. As Deborah Tannen points out, the Japanese have a different understanding. "Americans believe that spelling everything out in advance lays the foundation for trust by ensuring there will be no misunderstanding down the line. To the Japanese, trust is a prerequisite for working together; if there is trust, details will be worked out as they arise. Trying to spec-ify everything in advance shows that there is no trust—and no basis for a work-ing relationship."[4]

Based on this growing body of literature—where trust is both a social and an economic virtue—it could be tempting to speculate that relationships of trust between African governments and donor governments are impossible ei-ther because of radically differing definitions of trust or because of the low levels of trust inherent in African societies. On closer examination, these ar-guments don't hold up to scrutiny. Despite differing concepts of trust, Japan-ese and Americans are managing to conduct increasing volumes of business together, learning as they go along. There is no reason that the same dynamic cannot apply to donors and African governments.

There is also no reason to believe that the donor countries have a monop-oly on trust. While the rule of law and clearly regulated business relationships may be partially or totally absent in many African countries, cooperation, trust, and community are deeply held values in traditional African society. In Mozambique, for example, despite a long civil war, rapid economic changes, and continuing regional tensions, when asked the question, "Generally speak-ing, would you say that most people in your country can be trusted, or that you can't be too careful in dealing with people?," 88 percent of the respondents replied that people can be trusted.[5]

At the same time, there is evidence that there may be declining levels of trust and social capital in some of the more advanced societies, particularly in the United States. The exponential increase in litigation, a decline in volun-teerism, and the lack of stable social structures in many urban communities all point to a decline in social capital.[6] Many Africans would argue that social capital and trust are increasingly scarce commodities within many of the donor nations.

Finally, some may have the view that a true relationship of trust cannot be established in a situation of inequality, such as that prevailing between African governments and donors. While inequality can make trust more dif-ficult to achieve, it is not impossible. To begin with, it is a fallacy to believe that African governments are entirely powerless in the aid relationship. They understand that donor nations have a lot at stake and that donors cannot just walk away—both because of the vast sums already invested and because of the imperatives of globalization (not to mention humanitarian reasons)—

except under extreme circumstances. This knowledge gives African governments considerable leverage just as money gives donor nations leverage. As one European ambassador succinctly put it: "Mozambique needs us and we need a successful Mozambique—and they know it." But trust is not about equal leverage. Trust is precisely about overcoming the need for strictly rational calculations or quid pro quo ("tit for tat") in relationships. We have all seen true examples of trust between parent and child, teacher and student, employer and employee.

So despite a number of complicating factors affecting both donors and African countries, there seems to be at least a minimal basis for establishing relationships of trust—and trust is the foundation of influence. If I trust someone, I am more apt to be open to what they are saying. That doesn't mean that I will automatically do what they say. But over time, if there is a continuation of dialog and trust—and the arguments make sense—I am likely to absorb the other person's point of view and maybe even adopt it as my own. This is far more likely to happen than if the same point of view were imposed upon me. In addition, where there is trust, there is room for the relationship to become a two-way street. The other person is open to listening to *my* views and what I have to say may change *their* mind.

### CONDITIONALITY
Without belaboring the point too much, rational arguments and calculations alone are unlikely to work in isolation from trusting relationships. In the last two decades, the aid business has tried to substitute rules and conditions for relationships and trust. And as Fukuyama succinctly puts it, more rules equal less trust. "There is usually an inverse relationship between rules and trust: the more people depend on rules to regulate their interactions, the less they trust each other and vice versa."[7] While critics of aid see the imposition of conditions as the blatant exercise of power, the proponents of conditionality argue that nothing succeeds like success. If you can get government officials to do the right thing, they will see by the results that it was the right thing to do and become convinced that they did the right thing. For others, it's even simpler: aid agencies exist precisely to impose conditions and reduce a country's degree of freedom in the use of aid funds.

There are problems with this approach. First, the use of rules and conditions has absolutely no chance of success unless it is clear what the "right thing" is.[8] Given the complex environment in Africa, the "right thing" is seldom evident. During most of the last thirty years, donors have been the prime force behind project and program design, and in many instances, implementation. As President Obasanjo of Nigeria once remarked, "In education and in industrialization, we have used borrowed ideas, utilized borrowed experiences and funds, and engaged borrowed hands. In our development programs and strategies, not much, if anything is ours."[9] And there is little debate that the donors' track record, while enjoying some successes, by and large has been abysmal.[10]

But even if it is the right thing to do, the coercion inherent in most forms of conditionality engenders resentment and gets in the way of lasting change. In most African countries, debate on policies seldom focuses on the substance itself. Instead most of the debate is immediately hijacked into a discussion of whether or not the policy was forced upon the country by the IMF, World Bank, or some other donor. No matter what the policy, more often than not, it is the kiss of death if a policy change is seen to be the result of external pressure or conditionality.

Proponents of conditionality argue, with justification, that given the absence of mass democratic institutions in African countries, conditionality sometimes serves to protect the interests of the poor against a privileged elite. This certainly seems to be the case where donors have argued for more funds for primary education by cutting expensive subsidies for universities that serve only the privileged few, or when donors defend higher prices for poor farmers against the interests of a minority of urban consumers or food processors. But where the relationships between donors and governments and civil society are mainly formal, distant, and riddled with suspicion, it is relatively easy for privileged elites to manipulate public opinion even on these kinds of issues. It doesn't take much to convince a suspicious public that the true motivation of donors is to sabotage the university and industry in order to keep the country poor, backward, and a continuing source of cheap labor and raw materials. Never mind that in our increasingly complex, technocratic, and knowledge-based world economy, cheap labor and raw materials are not nearly the advantage they once were.

It is reasonable for donors to expect certain things in exchange for the foreign aid they provide. The question is whether there is a way of doing this that helps to build trust instead of undermining it. Because even where conditionality has succeeded on a particular issue, the costs are enormous. The drafting and negotiating of legal contracts and the ensuing monitoring and enforcement impose considerable burdens on African governments and donors alike. This is what economists refer to as "transaction costs." And there definitely is the syndrome of winning the battle and losing the war. Both donor and government credibility may be seriously harmed by the widespread belief (or reality in some cases) that donors forced an issue and the government did not have the courage or ability to resist. This makes policy changes all the more difficult in the future and serves to undermine the donors' image and their influence—as well as that of the government. Once in this situation, it is difficult to reverse and can easily lead to a worsening of the relationship between the donors and the government as the government struggles to demonstrate its autonomy and restore its credibility.

## ELEMENTS OF TRUST

How can donors change this dynamic and build trust? There is no magic formula. When looking at the aid setting, there seem to be at least six key elements that are important for a trusting relationship: some extent of shared purpose; commitment; reliability; familiarity; transparency; and honest and open communication. Some might add respect to this list. When asked about the aid relationship, people frequently speak about the need for respect—about as frequently as they talk about the presence or absence of trust. But respect doesn't create trust. When there is no interaction between two parties, respect and trust are two different concepts. For example, I can respect someone I don't know for their accomplishments without having any notion about whether I can trust them. When two parties have an interactive relationship, as is the case in the aid setting, the relationship between respect and trust is a bit more complicated—they are inextricably linked. Without trust, there cannot be true respect in a relationship. You can be courteous to and perhaps even admire or fear someone whom you don't trust, but it is impossible to truly respect them. And if you trust someone at least on one dimension, for example the professional dimension, a certain degree of respect is incorporated into that trust. Unlike the basic elements that help to create trust, respect emerges organically where there is trust. So when we speak about trust, respect is embodied in that concept. Let us now explore how each of the basic elements that create trust plays itself out in the aid relationship.

### Shared Purpose

Common goals and purposes are powerful tools in creating trust. This has been increasingly recognized by businesses worldwide that have created mission statements or vision statements in an attempt to provide a platform for trust and teamwork among their employees. As an example, the vision statement of the World Bank is:

> Our dream is a world free of poverty. Our Mission [is] To fight poverty with passion and professionalism for lasting results. To help people help themselves and their environment by providing resources, sharing knowledge, building capacity, and forging partnerships in the public and private sectors. To be an excellent institution able to attract, excite, and nurture diverse and committed staff with exceptional skills who know how to listen and learn.

The theory behind vision statements is that if we have a "common compass," then we can have a diverse set of activities going on at any particular moment, but still have the ability to relate specific tasks, however mundane, to the overriding purpose or goal. An overarching common purpose can help people feel that they are all in the same boat, rowing in the same direction.

To what extent do donors and African governments share a common purpose? The question is not as easy to answer as one might suppose. On a formal level, the answer is perhaps clear—donors and African governments are united in their objectives to reduce poverty and human suffering and bring prosperity to the citizens of Africa. This should provide a common platform for coordinated action and trust.

At the individual country level, this answer is far from obvious. In the countries we have termed "uncertain reformers," donor and government representatives are likely to give a positive response when asked, "To what extent do donors and the government share a common purpose in this country?" This was confirmed in interviews I conducted for this book in two southern African countries, Mozambique and Zambia, that are typical "uncertain reformers." Yet, for both donors and government officials, there are powerful influences that undermine this shared vision. Both frequently will elaborate: "We share a common objective, but we differ on the specific steps and timing of how to get there." The political realities and pressures faced by African governments frequently dictate different courses of actions than those recommended by donors. Many times, donors interpret this as a problem of *political will* ("If they really wanted to do it, they would do it and manage the consequences"). In turn, this begets a suspicion that there *really* isn't a common purpose. And African officials, for their part, are left with the impression that donors don't understand the realities on the ground, and even more damaging, that donors don't trust them.

Who's right? The unsatisfying answer is that both are right—to a greater or lesser degree, depending on the circumstances. And these circumstances are growing increasingly complex in many African countries. With noted exceptions, many governments, with strong urging and support from donors, are moving in the direction of more open and democratic societies. But this means that on many issues an increasingly vocal and visible opposition can curtail government executive action, sabotaging or delaying reforms. Governments now have to take the political calculus into account. Many donors are not well versed in the political economy of the countries or have a fairly superficial understanding, particularly in those countries undergoing rapid political transition. And many governments—particularly those in transition from previously autocratic regimes—are reluctant to openly admit that their power and scope of action are now circumscribed by an increasingly active opposition. In moments of candor, both government and donor officials will admit that reform seemed easier in the "good old days" when one party rule or military governments enabled quick and decisive action. Easier? Perhaps. Effective and sustainable? Hardly.

Obviously, this is only half the picture. In a number of cases, emerging democratic processes are helping to strengthen the hands of both donors and governments in proceeding together on common goals. For example, there has been a broad coalition of both local and international nongovernmental organizations (NGOs) lobbying for debt relief. In Mozambique and a number of other countries, this lobbying has played a role in bringing about faster, deeper debt relief *and* in ensuring that the money saved from debt service payments is directed toward substantial spending increases for education, health, and other services directed at the poor. Democratic openness is also helping to ensure that reform, once pursued, is more difficult to reverse. The broad-based support for moving away from a state-dominated economy in Zambia may well be the key element in explaining the survival of the economic reform program throughout the 1990s, despite many setbacks and wrong turns and nearly impossible circumstances, including a failing copper industry and a fairly hostile donor/government relationship.

Complicating the issue of shared purpose is the fairly obvious point that both donors and governments have multiple and sometimes conflicting objectives. As mentioned in chapter 1, donors frequently have commercial or security/strategic interests that color or determine their aid policies. In the Cold War era, when keeping Soviet interests at bay was judged paramount, in a number of countries eliminating poverty was not foremost in the minds of key donors nor the governments they supported. Carol Lancaster makes the point that much of the U.S. aid to Africa during that period was wasted, from the standpoint of achieving economic development, on failed or collapsed states (e.g., Somalia, Liberia, Zaire).[11] With the new emphasis on the links between security concerns and aid following the World Trade Center attacks and the Iraq war, there is at least some danger that history will repeat itself.

Commercial interests also continue to be an important element of some countries' aid policies. These interests may not necessarily undermine a shared economic objective, especially where foreign businesses are helping to bring about economic development. However, there are also clear cases of conflicting objectives, particularly surrounding tied aid. Tied aid is when donors provide aid that can only be used to purchase goods and services from the donor's country. It is a practice that the Organization of Economic Cooperation and Development (OECD) has tried to discourage, but many donors are reluctant to untie aid, not the least because benefiting companies, acting out of self interest, have tended to be strong supporters of foreign aid. Untying aid could result in loss of support for the overall aid effort. Nonetheless, tied aid has been associated with inappropriate goods and construction projects, as well as ineffective technical assistance. In addition to its questionable impact, tied aid lends credence to developing countries' complaints that donors do not necessarily have the best interests of the recipient in mind. It undermines commonality of purpose and trust.

Governments and government officials also have multiple objectives, some of which can and do conflict with poverty reduction and economic development. The most obvious one is maintaining power for the current government. Unpopular reform measures, however beneficial to the poor, are unlikely to be adopted if powerful interests object and there is a serious threat to the stability of the regime or its electoral prospects. In additional, personal objectives, such as getting rich quickly or moving up the career ladder, can dominate more noble purposes for both governments and donors. Also, in relatively young and weak nation-states, the government can hardly be seen as a monolithic, unified entity, speaking with one voice. When I asked both government officials and donors about the extent to which the government and the donors have shared objectives or purposes, a number of respondents' first reply was: "Who is the government?" This is not the place for a treatise on the nature of the modern state in Africa. So suffice it to say that the coexistence of modern states alongside traditional governing structures, the multi-ethnic nature of most African countries, and the relative newness of the state "machinery" make it difficult for most African governments to pursue clear objectives.[12]

Given all of these factors, shared objectives between governments and donors cannot be presumed to exist. And formal statements alone will never tell us much about the extent of shared purpose between a government and its donors. Needless to say, the extent of common objectives will vary substantially from country to country and over time. So what does this mean for trust? If common objectives are genuinely shared, this is the strongest platform for trust. However, trust can also exist when objectives are not completely overlapping, but there is complementarity. Ambitious politicians, especially if they see their own reputation as bound up with a successful reform program, can become champions of reform and develop close relationships with donors. Promoting foreign direct investment can serve commercial interests abroad, while creating jobs and increased prosperity in Africa. In these cases of complementary objectives, trust is not automatic or permanent, but there is sufficient compatibility for trust and productive relationships to exist.

On the other hand, where objectives are truly in conflict, there is little hope that a productive relationship can be established between governments and donors. This is particularly the case when one party or the other is more interested in personal gain or career enhancement than economic development. While morally reprehensible, it is easy to see how these circumstances develop. For both government and donor officials, in a world filled with uncertainty and disappointments—coups, natural disasters, civil wars, AIDS, worsening poverty—it is not uncommon for optimism to give way to cynicism. Dreams of a better society evaporate into a focus on winning the next election, getting the next promotion, or gaining some personal security for one's family.

## Commitment

To some extent, commitment is related to the existence of common objectives. Few people consider commitment a positive feature unless the commitment is to a cause or purpose they can relate to or agree with. It does not necessarily follow, however, that if there are shared purposes you can take commitment for granted.

Commitment is hard to measure, because it is subjective, emotional, and passionate. It can be among the most powerful factors in creating trust and can actually help to overcome or counteract other negative influences on the aid relationship. When you listen to African officials and donors talk about factors that influence their decision-making and the aid relationship, the word "commitment" crops up time and time again.

It's useful to distinguish two types of commitment—institutional and personal. Both are important in building trust. Donors are continually trying to measure the extent of commitment that African governments have to economic and social reform programs. There seem to be at least five key ways that donors try to measure institutional commitment.

*Boldness*    The first measure of institutional commitment is making some judgment about the boldness and pace of reform. The bolder the moves or the quicker the pace, the more the government is seen to be proving its commitment to reform. It is unquestionably a macho view of reform. While questions about sustainability may be quietly asked, the answers usually don't affect the judgment much.

*Compliance with Conditions*    The second measure that donors look at when judging commitment is compliance with conditionality: "Are they living up to their promises?" Possibly because there is a predilection for "bold reform," there seems to be an accompanying tendency to underestimate political difficulties, overestimate implementation capacity, and downplay differing objectives when formulating conditionality. Other donors tend to view the World Bank as the leader in "excessive optimism," but it is by no means alone. Not surprisingly, compliance with formal conditionality has not been particularly good.[13] And when conditions are not met, even when difficulties related to political circumstances or capacity are acknowledged, the inevitable label of "mixed track record" gets attached to judgments about the government's commitment to reform.

*Signals from Officials*    A third measure that donors use to judge commitment is by interpreting signals received from senior officials. Because of this need, donors, from ministers of state down to technical team leaders, want direct face-to-face access to senior government officials. This places an enormous burden on those officials. In a country like Mozambique, during the course of a year there are dozens of visits from senior ranking aid officials and politicians. This number explodes when the literally thousands of appointments sought by project teams and local aid representatives are factored in. Despite this overload, many donors still consider the unavailability of senior government officials as signaling a lack of interest or commitment. Furthermore, unless the senior official verbally expresses a strong commitment to the specific set of reforms currently under discussion, donors are likely to come away with—and share with other donor colleagues—a sense of "lukewarm commitment." Interestingly, African governments usually welcome these visits by senior aid representatives and interpret them as public signs of support and commitment on the part of the donor.

*Privileges and Status Symbols*   A fourth measure donors use to assess institutional commitment is by judging the appropriateness and consistency of government "perks" and celebrations. Many donors view governments that provide their ministers with Land Rovers or Mercedes (different countries have different status symbols) and allow their officials to take numerous official trips abroad as less committed to a development and poverty reduction agenda. Large offices and private bathrooms also have a jarring effect, particularly in ministries that are decrepit and dirty, with elevators that don't work. Similarly, national celebrations or national monuments that are perceived to be overblown can throw a pallor over the perception of government commitment. In the past, these elements were seldom mentioned in an official context, but consciously or unconsciously, they tended to color donors' views of "the seriousness" of the government. Increasingly, these issues are a part of the official dialog. In November 2000, after donors in Malawi got upset over the purchase of a fleet of new Mercedes for government ministers, the president of Malawi not only put the Mercedes up for sale, but dismissed the entire cabinet to show donors that he was serious about fighting against ministerial privileges and corruption. He subsequently reinstated many of the ministers, but the point had been made.[14]

*Public Statements*   Finally, public diplomacy plays a role in donors' assessment of government commitment. Donors constantly look for references in public speeches to what they consider to be priority actions. Whatever the topic—be it AIDS, corruption, civil service reform, or privatization—donors suspect weak commitment unless it is publicly pronounced—and hopefully more than once—to be a government priority. Several years ago, I was asked to review key speeches (e.g., the annual budget speech or the opening of parliament) by the prime minister, president, or minister of finance to count how many times the word "poverty" appeared. The theory behind the request was that the more a government was talking about poverty, the more it was doing about it. Maybe, maybe not.

There are obvious problems with this type of subjective assessment of commitment. For one, it generally fails to consider political, social, or cultural realities that may be at odds with European and American notions of behavior and commitment. And some African governments have become very good at "playing the game," independently of the strength of their commitment to reform. These instances of feigned commitment undermine trust and tend to strengthen the case of those who believe that firm conditionality and its enforcement are the only way forward in the aid relationship. Faking commitment not only directly eats away at trust, but also strengthens the perceived need for tighter conditionality. It's easy to see how vicious cycles get started.

African governments also make judgments about the extent of donor commitment. Obviously, the amount of aid, and whether the aid is trending upward or downward, is perceived as an important measure of commitment. There is one nuance here. Most of the fanfare and data refer to the amount of aid pledged or allocated by a donor in any particular year. For some donors, the amount of aid actually spent is close to or even exceeds the allocated amount. Other donors consistently fail to provide the amount of aid promised. African governments tend to look at the amount of aid actually received and the timeliness of that aid as the better measure of commitment. In some cases, delays are actually more a function of bureaucratic problems than flailing commitment, but it doesn't seem that straightforward to most African governments. As one senior government minister said to me: "When there are delays, they build on the impression that the donors are not well-meaning. Sometimes, the delays give the impression of a shifting of the goalposts, or that donors are just waiting and looking for mistakes."

The amount of money is not the only way that African governments measure donor commitment. The perception that a donor is willing to give the government the benefit of the doubt when things get tough is perhaps more important than the money itself. Donors that have a longer relationship—and one that is not prone to crises and aid stoppages—are viewed as the most committed. By contrast, donors who engage in a start-stop pattern of aid are viewed as "fair weather friends," not to be counted on—or trusted. Donors that try to work with governments on possible options to resolve thorny issues are considered to be more committed than those that merely present conditions and walk away, returning when conditions are met or alternatives are proposed. The latter approach, justifiably, may be viewed as less paternalistic and more businesslike. But African governments tend to see this as "cold-blooded." For them it represents a donor's reluctance to roll up its sleeves and work with the government on feasible solutions that everyone can live with. Not all, but many technical teams, especially those that fly in from far away, tend to use this approach. Governments conclude that they are callous, detached, and not committed to the country's welfare. It is not just the substance, but the style of work that creates tensions precisely because it is seen as a measure of commitment or the lack thereof.

All of the above refers to institutional commitment, but perceptions of individual or personal commitment also have substantial weight in the aid relationship. And because emotions are attached, these can, in some instances, be even more damaging to establishing and maintaining trust. On the one side, signs of material wealth—Rolex watches, Mont Blanc pens, and expensive suits—almost inevitably lead to suspicions that a minister is siphoning funds for his or her personal use or engaged in other forms of corruption, regardless of the person's economic status prior to assuming office. Tales of drunkenness or inappropriate conduct on the part of government officials—some true, some false—make the rounds quickly through local donor communities. Ironically, the same kinds of issues and personal behaviors lead government officials to call into question the personal commitment of donor representatives. The exotic holidays and comfortable lifestyle of many donor representatives who live in the country—and it is not uncommon that it is a lifestyle materially superior to that they would have had in their home country—reinforce a perception by government officials that some donors are enjoying a paid holiday, with no real stake or interest in the country's future. It is hard for country officials to acknowledge that some of these material perks are necessary because it is difficult to get high-quality donor staff and their families to live and work in poor and often conflict-ridden environments. This topic gets even more convoluted. When donor representatives attempt to dispel notions of hierarchy and avoid outward signs of wealth and status by, for example, dressing casually, they are generally resented by government officials, who view this as a lack of respect and another symbol of a lack of seriousness.

Are these perceptions fair or unfair? Any donor or government official working in the aid business probably has a dozen anecdotes that can reinforce the notion that personal attitudes and behaviors exist that demonstrate a lack of commitment and undermine trust. At the same time, most in the aid business can also relate a series of anecdotes testifying to personal commitment. In my own arsenal of anecdotes, I can readily recall ministers who travel for weeks on end, arrive late at night, and are back in their offices by seven the next morning to meet the next visiting delegation. I also recall donor representatives who missed birthdays, anniversaries, graduations, and even funerals while on official travel; and government officials and donors negotiating aid packages over Easter and Christmas, spending holidays far from home. There are plenty of sleepless nights, failed marriages, and neglected children on both sides.

The point is that perceptions of both institutional and personal commitment are highly subjective, but once formed, they are hard to dispel. Both government officials and donors tend to assume that the extent of their commitment is plainly obvious. Often, it is not.

### Reliability

Being reliable is another basic element for building trust. Nothing undermines trust more than broken promises and erratic behavior. Much has been written about the failure of African governments to live up to their reform commitments. Less has been written about the reliability of donors.

African governments tend to view some donors as more reliable than others. But most, if not all, donors have problems being totally reliable even in situations where the government is faithfully continuing its reform efforts. The first issue is the time dimension. There are certainly instances—usually connected to emergencies—where donors rise to the occasion and provide assistance immediately. But on the whole, governments complain that project approvals and release of funds generally take much more time than originally planned. They emphasize that the delays constantly throw government plans into disarray and make it harder for the government to live up to *its* commitments.

There is a good deal of merit to this argument. As noted earlier, some donors pledge aid, but never disburse it or disburse it only after long delays. Some of the European countries have adopted rapid, decentralized approval procedures that have reduced delays, but in many aid bureaucracies, project approval still takes a long time—in some cases, two or more years. No matter the projected length of the project approval process, it usually takes longer. Many aid officials will point to delays on the government's side, and while true, there are long delays on the donors' side as well. In many agencies, project approval procedures are complicated, and delays can and do occur at every stage. Compounding this there is unquestionably a "conspiracy of enthusiasm." Project officials from both donors and governments consistently underestimate the amount of time it will take to get a project properly planned, approved, and started. Ministers of finance and aid directors rarely delve into the details of individual projects, and they, in turn, make commitments based on what their technical teams are telling them. Subsequently, projects are delayed. Everyone looks unreliable and fingers start pointing. The aid agency doesn't want to look inefficient and blames the government. The government, which may even have made public commitments on when a project will start, blames the donor.

Officials from both aid agencies and governments have become used to this dance, and some have learned to compensate. For example, many bureaucrats use both a "formal" plan and schedule and a "real" plan and schedule. The formal plan is the one generated by project teams. The real plan takes the formal plan, builds in delays and is then used for budgeting and staff planning purposes. Despite these types of coping mechanisms, the inability to provide aid in a timely manner affects perceptions of reliability and undermines trust.

The perception of changing conditions and evaluation criteria ("moving the goalposts") is even more damaging to reliability, and hence to trust, than the delays. Some governments claim that they never know where they stand with some donors. They feel that sometimes they meet conditions only to be faced with another set of conditions. They look at neighboring countries and judge that they are being held to different, higher standards. They look at larger countries on different continents and conclude the same thing. They cite examples where one representative of an aid agency tells them one thing and another representative of the same agency tells them something different.

Most aid agencies would refute those claims, but there is undoubtedly some truth to them. Being told different things by different aid representatives and having conditions added before project or program approval are common occurrences. There are several reasons for this. First, with some donors, communication among staff working on a country may be poor. Some staff may not be well versed on the latest positions. For others, different parts of a donor government may have different views, creating additional uncertainty and confusion. When confronted with questions, some donor staff, not wanting to appear ignorant or powerless, prefer to "take a stab in the dark" and hope for the best.

Adding conditions can be the result of several different factors. Donor technical reviews may determine that additional safeguards are needed to ensure project success or protect affected people or habitats. Policy reviews may determine that economic reforms are unlikely to yield expected results unless additional measures are taken simultaneously. But in addition to these technical reasons, changing conditions may also be the result of political pressures from outside the aid agency.[15] In the case of multilateral development organizations such as the World Bank, important shareholders such as the United States and Western European countries may insist on additional or changed conditions in order to allow program approval to take place. Although there are instances where management will oppose those changes, in many cases a compromise is worked out to allow the program to go through. Other aid donors may change conditions because of pressures from NGOs or because of different views held by other parts of the donor government. As for the charge that some countries are held to higher standards than others, most donors would agree. They emphasize, however, that they are reviewing performance in relation to the program that a particular government set out and the commitments that it made, rather than using one objective standard or a cookie-cutter approach to judge all countries.

The inclusion of good governance criteria (conditions related to political processes, human rights, and corruption) among the criteria or conditions by which a country's performance is judged has created further uncertainties. Over the years, donors have developed some clear and measurable economic performance criteria, but judging performance in the governance area is much more difficult and more subjective. There are many instances where governments claim to have met or exceeded relevant criteria, while one or more donors disagree. The donors may decide to withhold aid, and the affected government considers those decisions to be arbitrary and those donors to be unreliable.

Another dimension of reliability is the question of how a donor behaves when a government, for one reason or another, fails to live up to its commitments. A number of authors have argued that donors have generally declined to walk away even after conditions were not met.[16] Because donors don't mean what they say, governments also don't mean what they say. Unreliability is reinforced all the way around. In reaction, some donors have attempted to tighten both conditionality and the enforcement of conditionality. For good performers where reform is relatively advanced, this may not pose a problem. But for the countries I have called "uncertain reformers," the aid dialog generally degenerates into a series of deadlines or lines drawn in the sand. Given all the problems with formulating conditionality and the problems faced by "uncertain reformers," this does not result in a smoother aid program, more reliability on either side, a better relationship, or better results. Frequently, it ends up as a "stop-go" pattern of aid that is highly disruptive to development and reform efforts. Aid gets withdrawn for weeks or months until conditions are met. Both the African governments and the donors are thrown into an unpredictable situation that undermines trust and the relationship even further. For donors, there is the inevitable feeling of "damned if you do, damned if you don't."[17]

### Familiarity

Countless studies have pointed to the difficulty of establishing trust among strangers, and we know from daily life that it is much easier to relate to and trust people we know. The better we know someone, the greater the tendency to find similarities and commonality. Conversely, strangers, particularly if they come from different ethnic, economic, or cultural backgrounds, make us feel uncomfortable. There are dramatic differences in economic conditions, social norms, and cultural attitudes among donor nations and African countries. How does one begin to bridge that gap and move people to feel sufficiently comfortable with one another to relax suspicion?

It's not so easy. First, the knowledge gap is big. In recent years, the World Bank has conducted client feedback surveys in a number of African countries. Time after time, "lack of familiarity with local conditions" stands out as an area where client governments see a need for dramatic improvement Although there are exceptions, most donor agency staff begin working in or with a country with *no* formal briefing on the country's history, social and political conditions, or cultural norms.[18] Economic development agencies generally provide some briefing on economic conditions, but diplomatic staff are much less familiar with economic basics. While there are exceptions, it is rare to encounter development agency staff who have more than the thinnest veneer of knowledge about local history and literature.

Complicating matters is the fact that the knowledge gap is unequal, with the donors suffering a distinct disadvantage. Many government officials and other African elites have traveled and studied abroad and have considerable familiarity with European and American history and culture.[19] Television, movies, literature, and more recently, the Internet, all spread the basic elements of European and North American culture to the four corners of the earth, including Africa.

How to even the balance? The first thing that inevitably comes to mind is to move donor officials to the countries they are working on. Unquestionably, living in a country promotes familiarity. Donor representatives, government officials, and the country's elite see and interact with each other on a frequent basis, practically daily in many of the smaller countries. Residents almost cannot help but absorb the culture and customs of a country. There is power behind this argument, and it has convinced many aid agencies to increase their field presence. For example, over the last few years, the World Bank has moved increasing numbers of staff, and even more notably, managers, to third world countries.

Does country presence, however, always translate into better relationships or deeper trust? The answer is no. In situations where there is already tension, it can make matters even worse. Why is this the case? First, having a large number of aid personnel on the ground opens the door for direct donor management or interference in the management of aid projects. While sometimes this is the overt purpose, in many cases, it is an unintentional result of enthusiastic agency staff members who want to be involved—and who have considerable time on their hands. Most of the staff involved in these activities would claim that they are not interfering, but rather are engaged in teaching and capacity building. Evaluations of this type of resident technical assistance generally have not been positive.[20] A number of donors, among them the World

Bank, have concluded that these arrangements are more likely to be capacity draining rather than capacity building. And this may be even more the case when the situation is not explicit or intentional. And what about trust? Suffice it to say that it's hard to build trust when you feel that someone is constantly looking over your shoulder.

There are, of course, exceptions. Many successful partnerships on the ground have paved the way for better relationships and increased trust between a particular donor and a government. Too often this doesn't happen because donor agency staff posted to Africa are inexperienced, mediocre, or motivated primarily by expectations of a comfortable life style. Few of the staff engaged in capacity building actually have pedagogical training of any sort. Unsupervised experimentation is also a problem. The use of Africa as a guinea pig has been mentioned time and time again by African governments as a major irritant in the relationship.

Furthermore, residing in a country does not guarantee familiarity. It is not unusual in countries with a relatively large aid community for most socializing to be done with and among donors and not with nationals of the country. The nationals who are included in those social circles are generally those who have ties abroad, either because of extensive travel or study outside of Africa, or through marriage. This "enclave life" may not be what donor staff expect or want, but it happens. In most African countries, there is a lively expatriate community, and it is easy to stay within its bounds, especially if there are few overtures of friendship from African colleagues.

At more senior levels, there are other pitfalls associated with residing in a country for a number of years. Loss of perspective is perhaps the most serious. This has commonly been known as "going native," but arguably there may be more cases of aid personnel "going anti-native" in these circumstances. Minor irritants of everyday life can begin to color the relationship on both sides. Gossip—much of it false—takes the place of careful analysis and dispassionate reasoning. Personalities clash and unfortunately affect decision-making. Moreover, governments, especially where tension is already present, may perceive that donor representatives and ambassadors are ganging up on them or going behind their backs to deal directly with the private sector and other portions of the public. In one aid-dependent southern African country in the mid-1990s, a group of ambassadors and heads of aid agencies jokingly referred to themselves as the "board of directors" and were deeply involved in the country's economic and political affairs.[21] Civil society representatives and some public officials started bringing issues directly to them.

While most donor representatives are dismayed when they hear that story, it is by no means uncommon (albeit without the title). Local donor representatives in most countries meet regularly for purposes of aid coordination, and direct contacts with civil society have increased markedly over the past decade, spurred on by "open door" and "client friendly" policies adopted by most donors. In a number of cases (Botswana and Zambia being two), governments at one point decided to deal with donors on a bilateral basis only, finding it unproductive to meet with senior local donor representatives in groups. Some governments have also tried to curb independent donor/civil society contacts, or at least insist that a government representative be present during those contacts.

The issues surrounding donor organization and contacts with civil society are complex, and we will return to them later. The point here is that in a particular country setting, especially where tensions already exist, proximity on a daily basis can lead to distorted judgments and misperceptions, as well as to actions by both donors and governments that undermine trust rather than building it.

While living in a country certainly can help promote mutual understanding and trust, there are a number of circumstances where it has had the opposite effect. At the same time, the alternative of frequent short visits by a constantly changing cast of characters from donor agencies also has major drawbacks. There is less continuity, an almost certain danger of political, social, and cultural ignorance, and far fewer opportunities to interact in less formal ways. There are many examples of donor agency staff, despite numerous visits to the country, having never spent a night outside of the capital city. On the positive side, there is less opportunity for micromanagement of projects and programs (although some energetic and misguided Washington-based World Bank staff have certainly tried) and for loss of perspective. Also, in a somewhat perverse fashion, the role of visitor leads to courtesies being extended, for example, invitations to African homes, that may actually result in more relaxed, social interaction between donor representatives and African officials than is the case for donor staff resident in the country.

From the point of view of gaining familiarity in a way that builds trust, there are no pat answers. It seems to be less an issue of location, and more an issue of training; clarity and consciousness about one's role; staff continuity; and incentives and opportunities for cultural, political, and social familiarization. We will delve more into these topics when we discuss culture and institutional incentives and constraints later on.

### Transparency

The aid business has tended over time to be a fairly secretive enterprise. It mainly has been the domain of executive branches of government, arguably the least transparent of the various branches. Over time, and thanks largely to pressure from legislatures and NGOs, information on aid allocations and use is more available to the public. While the pressure for more transparency started in Europe and North America, in recent years it has rapidly spread to the African continent.

Both donors and governments have tended to view each other's decision-making processes as somewhat of a "black box." Part of this impression relates to the sheer lack of timely information about decisions. In the not-too-distant past, key government and donor documents were kept confidential. They were not released to the public, and released with delays to each other, if at all. This included donor country strategy and programming documents, government budget documents, and major policy papers. For example, in the 1980s, many governments did not even know what World Bank loans were planned for the next three to five years in their countries. Even in the late 1990s, I remember one ambassador proudly showing me his country's programming document—in a European language that neither the African officials nor I could understand.

All of this is now changing. NGO and legislative pressure on donors has also translated into donors pressing governments to make more information public. As a result, most key documents are now released to the public as soon as they are final. In addition, many donors now hold consultations with civil society and government officials prior to finalizing strategy and programming documents. A number of governments have also moved toward public consultations on budget and policy matters. Public consultations are now mandatory for poverty reduction strategy papers, most commonly referred to by their initials—PRSPs. PRSPs are government documents prepared with the assistance of the World Bank and IMF and are required for debt relief, IMF program approval, and World Bank policy lending. In addition, at the donors' urging, many countries are now publishing not only annual budget plans, but also budget results against the plan.

The sharing of information between donors and governments, and between them and the public, is creating more transparency, but there is still plenty of room for improvement. Take PRSPs, for example. There is recognition that PRSPs are an improvement over previous policy documents that were written by IMF and World Bank staff without public consultation. Yet, there remains concern that consultations have been largely ad hoc and that different groups, depending on the country, have not been involved.[22] Also, the challenge remains of keeping the consultations and transparency going as PRSPs are updated regularly. There is clearly a danger of "PRSP fatigue."[23]

Despite the increased sharing of documents and information, governments and donors still feel that they are ignorant of each other's decision-making processes. Governments are reluctant to reveal the inner workings of the executive branch because of concerns over sovereignty and possible donor interference. Also, senior officials are understandably reluctant to make explicit their own role—often because it is either more circumscribed or more powerful than the donors think. There are instances where individual donor representatives come to know in precise detail the who, how, when, and where of a particular policy discussion and decision. But access to that knowledge is more the result of a trusting relationship than its genesis. For the most part, government officials are fairly tight-lipped about exactly how decisions are made, a cause for quiet resentment among some donors. Donor representatives feel they don't have enough information to make reasoned judgments about what a government will do on a particular issue and they don't feel trusted. In turn, they may grow increasingly skeptical about the overall quality of the government's decision-making.

Governments feel equally in the dark about donor decision-making processes. To some extent, this is just a sheer problem of information overload. Each donor has its unique bureaucracy and procedures. It is virtually impossible to keep on top of all of them—especially given the nearly continual reorganizations and procedural changes in some important donors such as the World Bank and European Commission. While there are donor representatives who are able to concisely explain to government colleagues how decisions are made and what procedures need to be followed, all too often donor staff don't have a clear picture either. Government officials frequently complain that they don't know whom to call when they have a problem with a donor.

This is still the case, but things are getting better. The World Bank recognized the problem with its organization and relationships with country clients, and in the second half of the 1990s created a new managerial position, country director. The country director is accountable for all World Bank activities within a given country and is supposed to serve as a "one-stop shop" for the government (and donor colleagues as well). Government officials have been uniformly positive about this change. The standard comment is: "At least now we know who to talk to," but there is, however, the implied "even if we still don't know how decisions actually get made and by whom." Also, with more decentralization and delegation, many—but not all—local aid agency representatives and ambassadors are serving a similar gatekeeper function. In those cases, ambassadors can make quick decisions and provide almost immediate responses to the government.

There are at least two areas surrounding the issue of transparency that threaten to bring new tensions into the aid relationship. The first is the relationship between transparency and good governance. In recent years, donors have become increasingly concerned about the nature of the governments in Africa and have drawn a clear connection between what they term "good governance" and the prospects for economic development. In a nutshell, good governance means three things to most donors: increased government transparency and accountability, with checks on corruption and human rights abuses; political decentralization so that citizens throughout the country can have a say in government; and some form of multiparty democracy. All donors have increased their attention to governance aspects over the last decade, and for some, including Nordic countries like Sweden, it is becoming the single most important issue, serving as a litmus test for continued aid. The World Bank, by its founding charter, is prohibited from entering into the political aspects of the governance agenda, but has become increasingly active on anticorruption and government accountability.

It is not difficult to figure out why governance and related conditions have introduced new tensions into the aid relationship. Most senior government officials will readily admit a need for increased transparency and accountability in government, and NEPAD, the new partnership among African governments, has clear governance objectives. But governments are much more sensitive about specific charges of corruption. They will acknowledge that corruption exists, but there are different sensibilities as to how it should be treated in the public domain. After all, it could look like the government was out of control, a dangerous prospect for any African regime. Of course, incumbent governments are much less reticent when it comes to accusations against individuals associated with previous regimes. Officials are also sensitive about the extent and relative seriousness of corruption in relation to other pressing problems. It is difficult to accept lectures about corruption from "outsiders" who have not solved many issues related to corruption in their own, more prosperous societies. The human rights agenda faces similar sensitivities.

But much more serious than the tensions surrounding corruption and human rights is the second area: the tensions surrounding the more political aspects of the governance agenda. Governments view foreign donors as trying to micromanage "affairs of state" when they become involved in electoral processes and politics. In southern Africa alone, active pressure and threats to withhold aid have been associated in the 1990s with events such as holding municipal and national multiparty elections and engaging in discussions with the opposition. Altering restrictive electoral clauses in the constitution, changing processes for voter registration, and forming a government of unity by including opposition members in the cabinet have also been included in some donors' governance agenda.

The resentment surrounding the donors' role in domestic political affairs runs deep. African governments tend to view this as interference in their sovereign affairs and an attempt to turn African governments—within a very short time period—into cookie cutter Western-style democracies, with little regard for the country's previous history and political experience. They remind donors that political development in their own countries occurred over hundreds of years. For their part, donors cannot see continuing support for governments that continue to flout what they consider to be basic and universal human values—honesty in government, respect for human rights, and letting all citizens have a say (and a vote) in their country's affairs.

Increased transparency has ironically brought with it other tensions as well. With internal political changes, as well as pressures from donors, many African governments now have to consult major "stakeholders" or interested parties prior to undertaking specific reforms. In principle, this is to make sure that all those affected have an opportunity to voice their views to the government so that governmental decisions will have greater relevance and legitimacy. In theory, this is great. In practice, it frequently works against reform—especially reforms that benefit poor people while working against the vested interests of the prosperous (but highly vocal) few. In theory all stakeholders are consulted, but only the elite are able to clearly articulate their views and orchestrate organized opposition. In certain countries, this has slowed trade and market reforms that would have resulted in, for example, poor farmers getting paid more for their products.

In practice, democracy in much of Africa is still a democracy for elites, a situation that creates its own vicious cycle in the aid relationship. Donors push for more transparency and more public consultation on reform, but given the nature of most African societies today, public consultation and public debate are largely captured and manipulated by elites who will generally oppose reforms that thwart their self-interest. This opposition can—and has—caused delays and even reversal of reform efforts. Donors then get upset that the pace of reform is slowing or that the government is "backsliding." And governments get frustrated—and sometimes even suspicious that they are being set up to fail. Clearly, over time, as democracy strengthens its hold and there is fuller, more representative participation by civil society, this contradiction will tend to disappear. But in the meanwhile, it is generating additional tensions in the aid relationship.

On the whole, the move toward greater transparency has been positive and provides a platform for a more constructive relationship between African governments and donors. Transparency has brought with it pressure on the donors to make their own decision-making processes clearer, simpler, and faster. At the same time, the acceptance of the principle of transparency has gone hand in hand with political changes in African societies. In turn, these have created contradictions and new challenges for economic reform efforts —and for the aid relationship.

### Honest and Open Communication

It is a cliché to write that trust is founded on honest and open communication. Honest and open communication would seem essential for the aid business, where millions of lives depend on the understandings reached between governments and donors. But does such communication exist?

The answer is not a resounding yes, which is somewhat surprising given the communications explosion in recent years. When I first started working for the World Bank, telexes (typed on an electric typewriter and sent to a central cable office) were about the only form of fast communication. Telephone calls were expensive and of dubious sound quality. Between busy signals and calls not going through, it could take literally hours or days to get through to many third world countries. Letters, even those delivered by diplomatic pouch, took a week or more to arrive.

Contrast that with the situation today. Many aid officials can send telexes and faxes right from their desktop computers, while e-mail provides instantaneous communication. Letters sent either by fax or e-mail take only minutes to arrive. With the advent of cell phones, and their extensive use in third world countries to circumvent failing phone systems, it is now possible to reach ministers or aid officials anytime and anywhere—provided they've given you their phone number. And videoconferences now make face-to-face group conversations possible across thousands of miles.

But do more and faster communication options translate into *better* communication? Not necessarily and not very often. Why not? One factor is tied to familiarity. It turns out that some media, like the telephone or the videoconference, are difficult to use to discuss sensitive issues unless you know the other party fairly well already. And while e-mail and faxes have certainly helped communication flows, sometimes communication is *too* fast. There are countless examples of messages crossing and hasty or sloppy messages that actually create confusion.

The formality of diplomacy arose precisely out of a desire to avoid confusion or precipitous actions that could have disastrous consequences. In larger countries and most countries outside of Africa, there is generally a separation of functions between diplomats and development officials. In Africa, there tends to be a merging of the diplomatic corps and development agency officials. The reasons for this are straightforward. Since many of the countries are small, donor embassies are small, and some embassy staff take on dual functions. Second, in some cases (for example, the Nordic countries), the business of aid is the chief element in the relationship between the two countries, so it makes sense for the ambassador to be fully involved in the aid agenda. Third, some donor countries have placed aid agencies under the jurisdiction or direct control of the Ministry of Foreign Relations (Department of State in the United States), leading to a natural merging. Finally, in many small African countries, the aid business is "the best (and only) game in town"—diplomats become involved to avoid boredom.

Later on in this book, we will examine what this merging does to the substance of the dialog on aid and development. For now, we will concentrate on what this merging means for communication and communication styles. In many countries, it means that if an ambassador wants to see a finance minister or other economic minister, he or she needs to go through, or at least advise, the Ministry of Foreign Affairs (the counterpart ministry for the diplomatic corps). Meetings can be scheduled weeks in advance. It means that frequently the development business is conducted through the tools of diplomacy: "white papers" (position papers on a particular subject); formal letters to heads of state; and demarches (formal position statements delivered in person by an ambassador to a head of state). It means that even if a new ambassador is key to the development and aid agenda in a particular country, he cannot appear in public or at official functions until he has been formally received by the head of state. The development dialog takes on the rhythms of diplomacy—slow, formal, and deliberate. It's not much of a dialog, but rather more like a formal ballroom dance—two people dancing together, but apart. Keeping your partner at arm's length can be prudent, particularly if you are concerned about getting your toes stepped on.

In addition, the language of diplomacy gets mixed up with the language of development. African officials frequently complain that the donors don't speak plainly or honestly to them. They speak of mixed signals and misunderstandings. And both sides mistake the politeness and courtesy of a diplomatic encounter for consensus or agreement. This is compounded by the inherent inequality in the aid relationship. African officials are reluctant to come right out and say no to inappropriate programs, projects, and conditions, under the age-old adage that "you don't bite the hand that feeds you." African officials rationalize their lack of candor by saying that they don't want to offend the donors. They also cite instances when their objections are either not understood or brushed aside. Given the risks associated with speaking up, silence and inaction seem a more polite way to handle disagreement. After all, the costs of this strategy seem minimal, especially if what's being discussed is funded by grant money, money that doesn't have to be paid back.[24]

But in fact, the costs are considerable. Projects, whether funded by grants or by subsidized loans, use up the scarce time and resources of the relevant government agencies. Inappropriate projects or projects that lack government support divert attention from higher priority activities. When nothing happens or conditions aren't met, this sours the relationship. Donors can't understand why the government agreed to something but won't implement it, and the government gets labeled as one that doesn't keep its word or live up to its commitments. In some countries, such as Mozambique, the costs of silence in this type of situation are now acknowledged. As one senior government official told me: "We learned the hard way that sometimes we have to say no because there is no such thing as free resources. There really is no free lunch."

The inability "to speak truth to power" goes both ways. Just as many African officials are afraid to say no to senior donor representatives, many donor representatives and diplomats have trouble—beyond the rituals of diplomacy—in speaking candidly, especially to heads of state. One head of state complained to me that his meetings with some ambassadors were virtually a waste of time because the meetings were "not straightforward and businesslike," which is not so surprising. It is easy when speaking with colleagues to say, "I intend to tell the president such and such in no uncertain terms." This sort of frankness tends to melt away when faced with the protocol and trappings of power in the presidential palace. And most of the time, it melts away for good reason. When two human beings are face to face, it is hard to have straight talk if there isn't already a relationship, however fragile, with some modicum of trust.

Governments also complain that aid agencies, especially multilateral ones like the World Bank and IMF, err on the opposite side. They are too blunt, forceful, and undiplomatic. Many times, government officials are reluctant to allow aid representatives access to senior officials, prime ministers, and heads of state for fear that the conversation will be too blunt or critical. This is not just paranoia. There has been more than one occasion when ministers of finance or others have been so offended that they have walked out of a meeting.

Problems in communication also stem from differing mandates and decision-making authority. Aid officials sometimes do not have either the mandate or the information to decide an issue on the spot. When this happens they have several coping mechanisms. One is to be honest and say they need to consult higher-ups. This clearly shows the limits of their authority and brings with it the risk of being sidestepped or ignored in the future. Another option is to take a stab in the dark and make a decision and hope that subsequently (and quietly) it will be confirmed as the donor's official position. This brings with it the real risk of confusion and loss of credibility, particularly if the decision is wrong or reversed later on. A final—and common—way of dealing with this situation is to throw the problem back to the government by insisting on additional information, studies, or analysis. African governments increasingly have grown wary of these requests for additional studies or information. Sometimes the need is genuine; sometimes the requests are recognized for what they really are—stalling tactics or a less than direct way of saying no.

This issue cuts both ways. When I first started working in one African country, I found my visits extremely frustrating. I would arrive at the office of the minister of finance armed with a list of ongoing issues that needed resolution—the purpose of my visit. We would have a nice meeting, but there was little discussion other than clarification of what the issues were. Nothing would get decided, and I would leave. On my next visit months later, I would again arrive with a list of issues. Frequently, the meeting would revolve not around the issues I had brought with me, but those that I had raised in my previous visit. I joked with my staff that the government was always one meeting behind. It took me a while to realize that this particular government worked by consultation and consensus in the cabinet. The minister often couldn't respond to the issues I raised without discussing it first with his colleagues. After I realized that and began to respect the way in which that particular government worked, I was able to alter the way we worked with the government by allowing time between first raising an issue and expecting a decision. Our communication—and our relationship— became less fraught with frustration on both sides. Trust increased.

Finally, of course, there is the issue of language itself. As it happens, many officials on both sides of the table are not working in their native languages. This distorts communication. It is worst in the Lusophone countries because there are relatively few aid officials who speak Portuguese. Conversations, either with or without interpreters, are stilted, and there is considerable room for misunderstanding.

With all these impediments to honest and open communications, it is no wonder that people in the aid business frequently say that all the business gets done during lunches, dinners, and coffee breaks. Those are times when people can break through the barriers and rituals and have an informal and open conversation. In recognition of this, informal opportunities for conversation are systematically built into more formal occasions. For example, at consultative group meetings, long coffee breaks and a small dinner restricted to heads of delegation are now standard. And it does happen that sometimes two high-ranking officials, say a minister of finance and a director of an aid agency, manage to form a lasting relationship marked by informality, openness, and candor. When this happens, trust increases and makes a real difference in the aid relationship and how events play out on the reform agenda. But, unfortunately, these types of relationships are more the exception than the rule.

The whole question of communication is obviously complex, and this section has meant to merely introduce the topic as an important component of trust. We will return to the subject of communication and language in an intercultural setting later on.

## RECIPE FOR TRUST

Given all of the elements for building trust—shared purpose, commitment, reliability, familiarity, transparency, and honest and open communication—and given the constraints on both governments and donors in the aid setting, is it really possible to build trust? When looking at these basic elements in most specific country settings today, along with how aid relationships play out, there is not much room for optimism.

The elements for building trust, however, are not immovable objects—all of them can be changed, but are they all equally essential? Are some easier to "fix" than others? Without some extent of shared purpose, commitment, and reliability, it is simply impossible to establish trust. These three elements form the core elements for trust. The other three elements—familiarity, transparency, and open and honest communication—are more process oriented and can help build or strengthen the core elements, but they are essentially supporting elements. Without the presence of the core elements, no amount of familiarity, transparency, or good communication will produce trust (see figure 2.1).

The core elements for trust are harder to work on, can take a long time to establish, and can change rather suddenly. Among other reasons, this is because they are not wholly dependent on the dynamics of the government/donor relationship alone. Others, including the public in both donor and African countries, can influence these elements. Legislatures, special interest groups, or the general public can, at least to some extent, challenge objectives or establish new ones. They can also seek to change specific decisions. Coup d'etats, elections won by opposition candidates, and violent protests against higher food and gasoline prices are all examples where third parties can and have changed the extent of an African government's shared objectives with donors and its commitment and reliability.

On the donors' side, legislatures can unilaterally hold up aid allocations or determine new conditions or parameters for the relationship, thereby affecting a donor's shared purpose with a government and *its* commitment and reliability. Finally, for the core elements to take root, they must be founded on continuing interaction between the government and the donors. Donors cannot establish "shared purposes" by themselves, and both commitment and reliability—while perhaps coming from "within"—can only be established or clearly demonstrated through interaction.

In contrast to the core elements, the supporting elements are tools or techniques that less frequently, if at all, depend on the will of third parties (although third parties have created pressure for increased transparency, for example). In nearly all cases within aid agencies and African governments, there is considerable latitude to work on issues related to increasing familiarity, transparency,

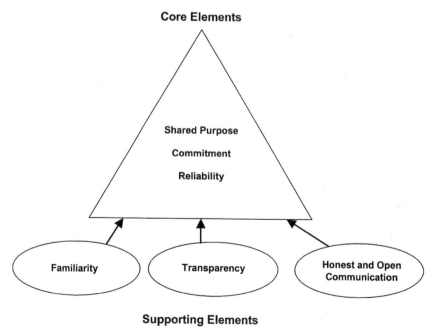

FIGURE 2.1
Basic elements for building trust in the aid relationship

and honest and open communication. While changes also require interaction to take root, there are more changes in these three elements that can be introduced unilaterally.

So where does one start? I am sure there are wise people out there who could establish the perfect sequencing, but I remember listening to a former minister of finance of Chile talk about his country's economic reform efforts. When asked about the appropriate sequencing of reforms, his answer was, "You do what you can when you can." That made a lot of sense to me, and that's my answer now.

You can start anywhere, but you can't remain working only on the supporting elements, because without the first three core elements, you will only travel part of the way. But in difficult relationships, increasing familiarity and cultural understanding and aiming for more transparency and honest communication may be necessary before you can even begin to talk about shared purposes and commitment. In other environments, a broad-based discussion of a country's long-term goals and prospects involving civil society, or working on specific administrative changes to improve the reliability in the relationship, may be the logical starting point. We will return to what can and should be done to improve trust and improve aid effectiveness in the last chapter.

Meanwhile, even with a determination to increase trust, there are many roadblocks in the way. In the next chapter, we will listen to donors and government officials from two southern African countries express their views and help us to discover which barriers to trust are the most important. As this chapter has shown, the list of potential barriers is long and could include cultural differences, communication skills, the ability to listen and learn, negotiation skills, personal and behavioral characteristics, and institutional factors. This may seem like a long list of things to overcome, and admittedly, it is a bit daunting. But some of these barriers are more important than others, and some are easier to remove than others. At least in theory, there are a number of things that can be done to increase trust, establish mutual influence, and increase aid effectiveness. The big question facing the international aid community is whether theory can be put into practice.

## NOTES

1. This should not be taken to the extreme. No donor was named that did not have an active aid program in the country. Once again, the argument is not that money isn't important, just that by itself, it's not enough.

2. Fukuyama 1996, p. 7.

3. There are a variety of definitions of social capital. This one is from Coleman 1988. See also Putnam 2000, especially pp. 19–24.

4. Tannen 1998, pp. 134–35. In this discussion, Tannen makes reference to Yoshiko Nankano, "Frame Analysis of a Japanese-American Contract Negotiation," Ph.D. dissertation, Georgetown University, 1995.

5. World Bank/Monitor Company survey (2000) of over 200 participants in World Bank country strategy consultations.

6. On this point, see Tannen 1998, especially chapter 5, "Litigation Is War"; Mosle 2000; and Putnam 2000.

7. Fukuyama 1996, p. 224.

8. There is a rich literature on the problems associated with conditionality, particularly in reference to structural adjustment. For example, see Killick 1997, White and Morrissey 1997, and Collier 1997.

9. Obasanjo 1987, p. 12, cited in Lancaster 1999, p. 3.

10. Lancaster (1999, pp. 159–60) points out that results from non-donor driven, government actions may not be better. "The lesson from the Swedish experience in Africa is that if 'donor-driven' aid is often ineffective, 'recipient-driven' aid can be equally ineffective."

11. Lancaster 1999, chapter 5, especially p. 94 and p. 111.

12. For a panoramic view of these issues, see Lewis 1998.

13. On this point, see Mosley, Harrigan, and Toye (1991) as well as the various reviews of adjustment lending by the World Bank. Because of the mixed record, there has been a concerted effort since the mid-1990s to have fewer and more realistic conditions for the World Bank's policy loans. Compliance among the countries that are currently most active in pursuing reforms, for example, Uganda, Mozambique, and Tanzania, has been good.

14. "Malawi and its limousines," *The Economist*, November 11–17, 2000, p. 60.

15. Lancaster (1999) reviews the relative autonomy of each of the donors she studies in her book and relates it to aid effectiveness.

16. Among others, see Stepanek 1999, especially chapter 7, Lancaster 1999, especially pp. 46–47, and Kanbur 2000.

17. The tragic consequences of this pattern of aid are highlighted in a 2003 *New York Times Magazine* article on Malawi. See Bearak 2003.

18. See chapter 6.

19. Although certainly less prevalent, this is even extending to Japan.

20. Among others, see Berg 1993 and Arndt 2000.

21. In addition to my direct knowledge, Lancaster (1999) also reports this (p. 68).

22. IDA and IMF (2002).

23. I am indebted to an anonymous reviewer of a previous version of this chapter for both the observation and the term.

24. Carlsson 1997, especially pp. 200–201.

# 3

# Barriers to Trust: Voices from the Field

If the key to improving aid effectiveness lies, at least in part, in improving the relationship between donors and African countries—as well as creating increased trust between them—then the last chapter tells us there's much work to be done. While it is tempting and all too easy for donor countries to "throw up their hands" and blame African governments for the failure of development efforts because of ignorance, incompetence, indifference, or malfeasance—or some combination—the preceding chapter begins to paint a different picture. Some of the basic elements needed to establish trust are sorely lacking or fragile *on both sides*. This has meant that the ability of donors and African governments to *mutually influence* each other has been limited.

The emphasis on mutual influence is intentional. If donor ideas, formulas, and know-how had been economically, politically, and culturally suitable for Africa, then successes in Africa during the 1970s and 1980s would have been more plentiful in that heyday of donor-driven aid programs. At the same time, results have been poor when nations have tried to go it alone either financially or intellectually. The interdependence of today's world and the imperative of rapid progress against disease and poverty mean that African nations need to borrow from the intellectual, cultural, and financial coffers of the donor countries. But the very nature of influence means that African countries can't and shouldn't be forced to take loans—be those loans of an intellectual, cultural, or financial nature.

As part of the worldwide concern linked to globalization, much has been made of the need to wipe out debt for the poorest nations. When it comes to the intellectual and cultural presumptions that accompanied the money, there also needs to be a clean slate. That is not to say that some of those ideas aren't good or even essential if progress is to be made, but they cannot be exported wholesale into the African context. They need to be blended thoroughly with elements of African political, cultural, and economic life. When I discussed globalization with a senior African official, he starkly pointed out that global-ization is unidirectional: "Globalization is trying to suck Africa into the West. They have defined the global view that contains little of African traditions and African conditions."

Success in Africa could well hinge on solutions that combine global views with African traditions and conditions, an approach that would return us to the need for true partnerships between donors and African governments founded on mutual influence and trust. This was confirmed by the interviews I con-ducted for this book with senior government officials in two southern African countries. I asked them why they had a better relationship with some donors than others and why some donors had more influence than others. They touched on many of the themes that are now familiar from the last chapter:

"The [European bilateral agency staff] are warmly received and treated. There's trust. When there's a real problem where we need support, that's where we turn."

"The [Multilateral agency] is influencing . . . there's a broader consultative process. It's a 'talking attitude.' Persuasion is subtle, so the locals feel like they are the ones initiating the ideas and actions."

"This country is like a beautiful twenty-five year old woman. The donors have to understand that just because she is young and pretty doesn't mean she can't speak for herself."

"I don't want the donors just to listen or put in money, but to discuss with us."

"It first has to do with trust, the trust that donors have in the leadership of the minister, if the minister is proposing realistic, reform-minded actions. It's also based on what has been the opening up of the government. We have decided to be open and sell our ideas—it doesn't cost anything to meet with the donors and discuss with them. The dialog that's established sometimes is not specific, but it increases shared vision and trust."

"The basis for the relationship has to be trust. But often there is still a lack of trust between headquarters staff and resident staff among the donors and between the government and the donors. Sometimes excessive protocol and the existence of two agendas hurt the relationship. What really helps is if the government has clarity in its agenda and is able to articulate it to the donors."

"A good relationship is one that gives space for each to see what the other thinks. It is formed on an ability to think and speak freely. There's great value placed on those donors you can go to and ask for something different, who are not afraid to experiment, who are not the ones who wait for the others."

"It's those donors that clarify positions in detail and that argue with us. Their people are authorized to discuss ideas and take positions."

The common theme running through these comments is striking. Discussion and dialog, faith and confidence—in other words, the opportunity and openness to influence each other's positions and views—were viewed as the foundation for trust and the building of a good relationship.

Not surprisingly, given this emphasis on dialog and interaction, personalities matter. Echoing throughout the interviews were comments such as, "Personalities play a big role on both sides. . . . Interpersonal relations make a real difference. . . . The [European bilateral] have had influence because of their ambassador who somehow reached our hearts." Many interviewees spoke of waxing and waning relationships based on the ambassador or donor representative who was in the country at a particular moment. But as one senior minister cautioned: "We like nice people, but they can't be banal. It's not just having a relationship for the sake of having a relationship."

Conversely, and as might be expected from the preceding comments, coercion, interfering with sovereign decisions, and having preconceived ideas were viewed as inimical to relationships, trust, and true influence.

"[Multilateral agency] is seen as a hostile party; you work with them under duress."

"Diplomats in this country overplay their roles as donors and underplay their roles as diplomats. . . . The concept of diplomacy is based on mutual respect.

The good diplomat respects sovereignty and allows you to work out your own priorities."

"What gets in the way is the question of determination of needs. Is it the needs of the donor or of the country that has precedence?"

"Sometimes I feel we are enslaved by the conditions at the macro level without being party to the discussions or sometimes even aware of them."

"There is some confusion in this country with the donors and the style of relationships. Ambassadors give their opinions on internal matters, including governance. We lose sight of the real role of ambassadors, which is to represent their countries. The donors use their money to pressure the government. The government has opted to tolerate this because of the poverty."

One might wonder whether the answers to these questions might differ significantly depending on the country and its present set of policies and relationship to the donor community. The two countries where I conducted the interviews, Mozambique and Zambia, are in some ways similar. Both are among the poorest countries in Africa, both are heavily indebted and aid dependent, both have a large group of donors resident in the country, and both have been implementing an economic reform program with massive financial support from the international community.

In other ways, they are a study of contrasts. Mozambique is growing steadily; Zambia is getting poorer. Mozambique is currently a widely acknowledged "aid darling," a favorite among many donors. It literally has offers of more financial support than it can successfully absorb. In contrast, Zambia has had a difficult and tumultuous relationship with its international supporters. Since the mid-1990s, bilateral donors have suspended balance of payments support during several extended periods because of dissatisfaction with issues related to political governance, fiscal management, and delays in the privatization of the national copper industry.[1] There have been periods when Zambia has been starved for aid and at the brink of defaulting on its foreign payments. In the minds of many donors, Zambia in the late 1990s and into the next century hovered on the edge of respectability when it came to aid decisions.

Given their contrasting experiences with the donors, you might expect that government officials in Zambia and Mozambique would have different perspectives on relationships with the donors, but they don't. Their answers were strikingly similar. I am sure that many of my colleagues would have bet money that the last quote on the role of ambassadors came from a Zambian official, but in fact it came from one in Mozambique. It signals that there is potentially "trouble in paradise."

How do the views of African governments on aid relationships match with those of donors? There are many similarities. While the donors tend to refer more often to the money and its role in the relationship, most recognize the importance of dialog and building relationships. Here's a small sampling of donor views from both countries:

> "It's about the money first, and the personalities next. Building trust is more important than strategic project selection—that's just too technocratic—for gaining influence."

> "There seems to be a reaction to the confrontational approach of the mid-1990s. Those donors with influence are working mostly in the background—they are less confrontational. . . . We are working on solutions in a quiet way. . . . We believe harsh words should be reserved. I guess old time diplomacy is back in Africa."

> "We try to adhere to government policy, not to be donor-driven—we listen carefully to their wishes. We hardly threaten with conditionality."

> "The influence from the bilateral donors is on the qualitative side. It's not about the numbers. The [European bilateral] take risks, they are innovative and propose new things. They are well liked, and they are not necessarily seen as weak. . . . They [another European bilateral] know what's wrong. . . . Despite this, they hang in there; they make it clear that they know; and the government knows they know. So there has to be trust in this situation. The government trusts them because they know, but they still try to help—and it doesn't show up on page one of the newspaper."

While donors struck the same chord as African governments for increased dialog and interaction, several of them voiced their concerns about a trade-off between country ownership and country-driven policies versus the need for rapid results and implementation of policies acceptable to donor nations and their citizens.

"There are three ways of using money to influence. The first is by saying 'do it or we'll walk away.' The second is 'if you do what we tell you, we'll help you finance it.' Both of these work in certain circumstances, but that's not what's working here. There's also a third way that says 'do what you want and if we like it, we'll finance it.' But that way doesn't get the government to move any faster."

"Let's face it. We are supply-driven salespeople. There is much talk about demand-driven aid, but it's not true. The moment a government says 'we need fourteen tanks,' we refuse."

"Our problem is: are we prepared to dialog and be flexible or do we just propagate and sell?"

For the donors, it is not only a question of doing what they think is right, but of the time involved. One of the donors told me that he had just watched a report on CNN in which the mayor of a small town in the United States defined the "haves and have-nots" by their access to the Internet. That seemed almost surreal to him because he was sitting amidst a population that lived on less than a dollar a day and where clean water was a luxury item. As one donor succinctly put it: "Can we afford to wait for the government to get its act together?"

The urgency of the situation in Africa is undeniable. But seductive as it may be, particularly to those with short attention spans—a characteristic shared by politicians the world over—exporting Western policies and programs wholesale into Africa and imposing change does not work. If living conditions for the vast majority of Africans are going to improve within a reasonable period of time, there seems to be no choice but to strengthen dialog and trust among the African governments and donors so that they are able to mutually influence each other.

### Measuring Trust

When it comes to building trust, how do the donors rate? In the interviews, I asked senior donor representatives in Mozambique and Zambia to rate the performance of their country or agency on familiarity with the country's culture, history, politics, and social structures; commitment; transparency; open and honest communication; and reliability. I asked them to use a 1–5 scale, with 5 being "excellent." You will recognize these as five of the six components of trust discussed in the last chapter, but they were not identified as such during the interviews.

This was not a scientific poll and one needs to be careful about reading too much into the responses or paying too much attention to the numbers.[2] Even with those caveats, the answers were interesting. The first thing that leaps out is that on all five items, donors rated themselves relatively high. The average score across donors was over 3.5 for all items. Commitment and open and honest communication received the highest ratings, averaging 4 or above in both countries. The donors saw themselves and their countries as being truly committed and engaged in "straight talk" with the two governments. Several government officials made the point that the trouble began when donors began to translate their commitment into action agendas and conditions that the government had to follow.

The items that received relatively lower ratings were transparency, familiarity with the country's culture and history, and reliability. Some donors readily admitted that they had agendas that were not completely out in the open. Others rated their transparency lower because of the complicated decision-making processes in their development agency or foreign ministry. The latter, combined with uncertainty about conditions imposed by parliaments or legislatures, also explained most of the concern surrounding reliability.

The question on how familiar the agencies were with political, social, historical, and cultural factors in the country was the one that drew the most varied responses. Well over half of the donors rated their agency or country as very familiar (4 or above), while only a minority questioned the extent of their knowledge (ratings of 3 and 2). It turns out that most donors apparently have a "blind spot" on this issue of familiarity. It seems that most donors think they know more than they actually do, at least according to government officials.[3] I asked the corresponding question to senior government officials, that is, how familiar do you think the donors are in general with your country's history, culture, politics, and social structure? There was some acknowledgment and appreciation of individuals who had taken the time to acquire this knowledge, but it was abundantly clear that most donors were considered to have superficial knowledge at best. The following are typical of most of the answers I received:

"The formal donors know almost nothing."

"Only the ones that employ local staff know something."

"There are few who can really see this country for what it is—a mosaic."

"They know very little. The donors see one big country of Africa, and all of Africa is seen in the same way."

"They are not familiar at all; the donors don't mix with the natives. . . . People in the villages are not worried about gender issues—they are worried about the basic issues of survival."

"It depends . . . some residents behave like 'tourists.' . . . [T]hey have no interest in the people, just the animals . . . sometimes you get interested people. Really good people tend to be interested. Others just sit in [the capital city], get drunk, and criticize."

Government officials tended to agree with their donor colleagues that commitment was high in the international community and that by and large communication was relatively open and honest. They were relatively less concerned about the transparency issue; most expected that the donors' decision-making and agendas would not be completely open to them. As one minister put it: "They are not transparent. They know everything that happens here, but we don't know what happens there. But that's not so important. What is important is that they fulfill their commitments." In other words, reliability was a key concern.

Here's what a couple of senior government officials had to say on the subject of reliability:

"Reliability is very important. One would like to agree on a set of goals and have the certainty that my partner will deliver if I deliver. In this respect, the multilaterals are the most reliable. Forget it with the bilateral donors."

"You can't make wild promises to high government officials and then nothing happens . . . it becomes a circus when they can't actually deliver."

And what makes a donor reliable? According to these officials, it's giving the government the benefit of the doubt, flexibility, and having clear and/or limited conditions for assistance.

"Those who have always been here are the most reliable; it's not so much about the money but about trust, confidence, and stability."

"There are donors who see that you are trying and give assistance as long as you are trying in good faith. Those are the most reliable."

"We view as most reliable those that offer to help, but that don't have conditionalities. They come with open hands and with few political consequences to using their assistance. . . . The ones that are least reliable are the ones that take the political temperature of the day and their support depends on that."

The Swiss, Japanese, and World Bank were singled out by more than one government official as being relatively more reliable donors. There were, however, differing perceptions of the degree of reliability that could be expected from the World Bank.

"With the World Bank, there are clear rules. Once you agree on the conditions and benchmarks, it's very clear."

"With the World Bank, it depends. The country director can be a shock absorber. . . . The country director can absorb donor pressure from the governments represented on the Bank's board of directors or transmit it back to the country."

The clear theme that emerged from these interviews is that more work needs to be done in familiarizing donors with the history, culture, politics, and social structures of the countries and on increasing the reliability of the assistance.

And how did donors and government officials respond in both countries when asked about the extent of shared objectives, the sixth component of trust? Their answers echoed the discussion in the last chapter. Most donors and government officials felt there was considerable overlap or sharing of objectives, at least in general terms. Most also felt there were differences—and at times substantial differences—in priorities, strategies, and timeframes. The interviews brought out several nuances. First, there is a thoughtful minority that sees little in the way of common objectives and relates this directly back to different worldviews and the impact of culture. A widely respected ambassador and an equally respected government official had this to say:

"We don't share objectives. My country is so affluent, and it has a consistent commitment to development. There's a Western, Christian orientation to human rights and good governance. Here, on the government's side . . . it's all about survival."—*Ambassador*

"We don't share the same objectives. There are different perspectives and definitions on what constitutes development. Some donors have interests that conflict with the government's development agenda."—*Senior government official*

A second nuance from the interviews is that both donors and government officials felt there was more congruence on economic perspectives than on political perspectives. Political governance was mentioned time and again as an area where the long-term vision might be the same, but where differences on what needed to be done and how to do it remained substantial. There was also the feeling expressed by one government official that there wasn't enough interaction and dialog to even try and forge a consensus. "There's so very little time for donors and the government to sit and evolve common views, or 'accepted ideas.'"

What emerges from the interviews on this question of shared objectives is on balance heartening. Although there remains some questioning of basic values and objectives, most people felt there was a good deal of shared, or at least, parallel goals. What is worrisome, however, was the extent of disagreement on *how* objectives should be reached, including the speed of change, particularly on issues related to politics and governance. Also troubling is the thoughtful minority that sees the cultural divide as almost insurmountable. It is an open question—at least for now—whether increased interaction would bring about increased consensus, or at least, increased understanding and trust. The interviews indicated that at the very least, there is some foundation to build upon—a critical finding given how fundamental some sense of shared objectives is for the building of trust.

So where does this leave us in terms of increasing trust, and thereby the possibility for mutual influence? What the interviews seem to indicate is that of the six components of trust, two of the core components—shared purposes and commitment—are present in sufficient quantity. The difficulties and disagreements, along with the fears and suspicions, emerge in the translation of vision into action. Problems associated with reliability and the lack of familiarity with the culture, history, and overall environment unique to each African country seem particularly intense, with issues of open communication and transparency somewhat less so. As a core component of trust, reliability poses particularly thorny issues. How do you trust someone you can't count on?

## Obstacles to Trust

While beginning to shed some light on the subject, that still doesn't tell us much about the actual obstacles to building a better relationship and increased trust. In the interviews, I asked donor and government officials what stood in the way of donors doing a better job in the country or having a better relationship with the government. The obstacle mentioned most frequently by government officials was their perception of donor interference in internal affairs and the donors' insistence on preconceived ideas and imported models. Personalities, institutional constraints on both sides, and specific conflicts related to political governance were also mentioned. For the donors, the most frequent responses zeroed in on disagreements over governance, institutional problems on the donors' side, and capacity problems of the government. A few government officials and donors talked directly about suspicions and fears and the need to build trust.

In addition to asking open-ended questions, I asked the people I interviewed to tell me which, if any, of the following, constituted an obstacle in the relationship: *culture and belief systems; communication and language; teaching, learning, and listening skills; negotiation skills; the personal and behavioral characteristics of donor staff; and institutional factors* (on both sides). I also asked them to rate the extent of the obstacle using a 1–5 scale, with 1 signifying no problem and 5 being an enormous obstacle. With these questions, I wanted to glean some specific insights on exactly what the problems were and how serious they were—a first step toward thinking about constructive ways to build trust and improve the relationship.

Once again, this was not a scientific survey or poll, nor did all the interviewees participate in the "numbers game," but a couple of things stand out from the numbers. Comparing government responses to donor responses, the government officials saw the obstacles as more severe. With only a couple of rare exceptions, government average responses were above 3, while donor average responses were below 3. Furthermore, there was basic agreement among the donors and the government officials *that culture and belief systems* and *institutional factors* related to bureaucratic problems in either the donors or the government were the biggest obstacles. This is striking, given the close relationship between these obstacles and the core components of trust that were considered to be the weakest: familiarity with a country's culture and history and donor reliability.

There were some differences between countries this time. In Mozambique, both government officials and the donors saw communication and language as a bigger obstacle than their respective colleagues in Zambia. This reaction is clearly linked to the fact that Portuguese is Mozambique's official language. Most of the time, conversations are taking place with either one party or both working in a second or third language. Under these circumstances, difficult communication—as well as miscommunication—is almost inevitable.

There were also interesting differences in the Zambia results. Compared to their Mozambican colleagues, Zambian government officials viewed personal and behavioral characteristics of donor staff and their own poor negotiating skills as much bigger problems. Zambian donors also saw these as relatively bigger obstacles than their Mozambican colleagues. Without reading too much into this, these responses seem to be a clear reflection of the tension and outright hostility that erupted from time to time between the Zambian government and members of the local donor community over the last several years. It may also reflect an acknowledgment by Zambian officials that they hadn't done a very good job in selling their viewpoint to the donors (i.e., negotiating). As one local diplomat said to me: "This business is all about impressions and perceptions, and Zambia is very bad at perception management."

Finally, some might expect that people interviewed in Mozambique, especially those in the government, would see the obstacles on the whole as being less severe than the people interviewed in Zambia. This would seem logical, given the perception (and reality—at least in terms of higher aid levels) of Mozambique's "better relationship" with its international supporters. Not so. Counterintuitively, the Mozambican government officials saw the obstacles as a whole as being at least as, if not *more* severe than their Zambian colleagues, and there was little appreciable difference in the intensity of responses between Mozambican donors and Zambian donors. Judging from these countries' responses and their differing status within the international aid community, it seems fair to conclude that problems in the aid relationship are fairly common and don't necessarily improve with higher aid levels. "Aid darlings" may come and go, but the problems stay, and possibilities for real progress, based on trust and mutual influence, remain untapped.

### Dialog Based on Trust

These interviews—"voices from the field," if you will—clearly validate the importance of dialog based on trust in the aid relationship. They also highlight the potential damage that coercion, perceived interference, and preconceived ideas can have on the relationship, drastically limiting the possibilities for mutual influence. The perceived trade-off in some donors' minds between rapid results and country-initiated or even country-endorsed policies seems remarkably shortsighted, given the dearth of sustained economic success on the African continent. And while there is no denying that capacity constraints exist, the interviews brought home that the real question may be "the capacity to do what?"

However, achieving mutual influence through building trust is arduous work. Based on these interviews, many donors seem to think they are doing a pretty good job on most of the core components of trust and tend to downplay the obstacles in the relationship. The African governments are far less sanguine. There is some agreement—not without some important dissent—on a sense of shared or at least, parallel objectives, and an even broader agreement on a high level of donor commitment and relatively open communication. Government officials point out, however, that most of the problems begin in the translation of broad objectives and commitment into concrete action agendas and conditions. Limited knowledge by donors of African cultures, histories, and political and social structures, combined with a series of institutional and political problems at home which affect the reliability of assistance, emerged as the key areas of donor weakness and again as the chief obstacles to building better relationships and improving aid effectiveness.

In the next two chapters, we will take a closer look at these obstacles, focusing on the role of culture and institutional factors that constrain donor behavior. Other elements—including intercultural communication, listening and learning, and negotiation skills—not to mention the role of personalities—will be woven into the discussion. The real question, of course, is what, if anything, can be done to overcome the obstacles. Answering that question is both difficult and controversial, but there's no escape. We will turn to it in the final chapter.

**NOTES**

1. Copper is Zambia's number one export. There are various types of aid, including support for specific projects, the provision of technical specialists, debt relief, and balance of payments or cash support. Governments particularly value the last category, balance of payments support, because it generally can be used flexibly to support government spending priorities.

2. The number of donors interviewed in both countries was twenty-four. The majority of the interviews were conducted at the ambassadorial or equivalent level, with some at the senior counselor level. Most of the interviewees were people I had met previously.

3. The number of senior government officials interviewed was thirteen. All interviews were at the permanent secretary level or above, with most at the ministerial or equivalent level.

# 4

# Culture Matters

It is difficult to write about culture and development and about culture and foreign aid. Culture is a touchy subject. As the sociologist Nathan Glazer said: "Before we resort to culture today to explain the differences in economic progress or political attitudes among nations and ethnic groups, we prefer to find other explanations. Culture is one of the least-favored explanatory categories in current thinking. The least favorite, of course, is race."[1] In the world of aid and development, culture is like the uninvited guest. You can't ignore it, but you don't really want to acknowledge it either.

One of the basic premises of international development is that there are useful experiences and knowledge that can and should be transferred from one country to another. Yet as we have seen from the previous chapters, African governments are wary of ready-made, imported solutions. While theoretically many of these "solutions" should work, often they do not. At the same time, international aid workers and diplomats pride themselves on being culturally sensitive and "feeling at home" in a variety of cultures. Here too there is a big disconnect. As we saw in the last chapter, donor representatives tend to think they have a reasonably good knowledge of local history, politics, and culture. On the other hand, their African hosts see a great deal of ignorance and cultural prejudice.

## DEFINING CULTURE

Given these differences, it's at least worthwhile to ask about the role that culture and cultural differences play in the aid relationship, as well as in establishing trust and improving aid effectiveness. Before diving into this, we need to define exactly what we are talking about. What is culture? As you might expect, there is a breathtaking array of definitions—maybe as many as 150.[2] There are narrow definitions, for example, referring to art, music, and literature or to a civilization's artifacts and rituals. But most definitions of culture are broader. Francis Fukuyama defines culture succinctly as an "inherited ethical habit" that can consist of ideas and values, as well as social relationships.[3] Richard Shweder, a University of Chicago anthropologist, is equally succinct: "What do I mean by culture? I mean community-specific ideas about what is true, good, beautiful and efficient." He goes on to say that those ideas must be socially inherited and customary, and they must "actually be constitutive of different ways of life."[4]

Without becoming involved in the intricate academic debates surrounding the definition of culture, the following definition from a text on intercultural communication captures the encompassing nature of culture that is relevant to the discussion that follows in the next pages:

> We define culture as the deposit of knowledge, experience, beliefs, values, attitudes, meanings, hierarchies, religion, notions of time, roles, spatial relations, concepts of the universe, and material objects and possessions acquired by a group of people in the course of generations through individual and group striving.[5]

No wonder most development specialists, apart from anthropologists, tend to sidestep cultural issues. "Economists, believing themselves to be the most hardheaded of social scientists, generally dislike dealing with the concept of culture: it is not susceptible to simple definition and hence cannot serve as the basis for a clear model of human behavior."[6] And economists are not alone: they are joined by their colleagues in finance, agronomy, and civil engineering, to mention only a few. Yet despite the complexities and qualms, it seems foolhardy to ignore culture and claim it plays no role in development and the aid relationship. Given culture's broad sweep, it surely must have an effect on notions of trust, communication, and conflict resolution; how people process information and learn; and how people relate to each other. But what exactly is that role?

## ROLE OF CULTURE

Not surprisingly, that question engenders a good deal of controversy and lots of legitimate worries. First, let's look at the controversy, which involves two schools of thought. The first is one we briefly alluded to in chapter 2. Boiled down to its essence, the argument is that certain cultures have characteristics that are more conducive to promoting human progress and prosperity than others. This intellectual trend, championed by social scientists such as Francis Fukuyama, Robert Putnam, Lawrence Harrison, Samuel Huntington, and a host of others, is known as "cultural developmentalism" and has led to a new interest in culture by economists and other development specialists. As you may recall from chapter 2, Fukuyama makes the argument that more economically advanced countries share higher levels of social capital and trust. Without these, he argues, it is difficult for nations to prosper. Others argue that the causality may be going in the other direction—that economic development is the cause of changing values. Ronald Inglehart, who has conducted cross-country surveys, claims that *both* are true: "Economic development seems to be linked with a syndrome of predictable changes away from absolute social norms and toward increasingly rational, tolerant, trusting, and postmodern values."[7]

This whole school of thought opens new avenues for development specialists. If cultural characteristics hold the key to human progress and prosperity, then the cultures of developing societies need to be studied and evaluated, with more attention placed on promoting shifts toward ideas and values that promote prosperity. Not so fast, argues the opposite school of thought, known as "cultural relativism" or "cultural pluralism." Many distinguished scholars argue that "cultural developmentalism" is the height of ethnocentricity, that Western values are being used to judge non-Western cultures. There are multiple definitions and paths to the "good life," and no one particular set of values should be used to judge others. Especially perilous are any attempts by "outsiders" to induce changes in values, customary practices, or other cultural characteristics as a way of inducing economic development.

The developmentalists claim that their position shows no ethnocentricity. On the contrary, all people seek prosperity, and there are certain "goods" associated with economic development, such as fewer children dying, that are universally desirable. Richard Shweder, a proponent of cultural pluralism, replies:

> I strongly believe in "universalism," but the type of universalism I believe in is "universalism without the uniformity," . . . In other words, I believe there are universally binding values but that there are just too many of them. . . . I believe that those objectively valuable ends of life are diverse, heterogeneous, irreducible to some common denominator such as "utility" or "pleasure," and that they are inherently in conflict with each other. I believe that all good things in life can't be simultaneously maximized. I believe that when it comes to implementing true values there are always trade-offs, which is why there are different traditions of values (i.e., cultures) and why no one cultural tradition has ever been able to honor everything that is good.[8]

Another anthropologist, Thomas Weisner, hones in on Africa and one important aspect of culture—child-rearing.

> In my view, there is nothing fundamental in the parenting and child care practices in Africa today that would prevent economic development under some version of a market model or a local version of a more pluralist society. Many values and practices of African family life and child care are at least compatible with economic development and political pluralism.[9]

In his view, the tight link between specific cultural traits and economic advancement is at best overstated: different cultural practices do not get in the way of economic development. And while not ignoring universal "goods," there are multiple paths for getting there.

> Cultures should be judged on their ability to provide well-being, basic support, and sustainable daily lives for children and families. I do not have a relativist stance with regard to these features of child life. . . . But we should leave it to the internal mechanisms of change and debate within communities as to how, with what specific content, and towards what cultural goals these three conditions should be achieved.[10]

Which side in this debate is right? It certainly isn't clear-cut, but there are a couple of things that are striking when looking at the debate in the context of economic development and the relationship between donors and African governments. First, depending on what side of the academic debate you are on, there are conspicuously different implications for economic development policy prescriptions and for foreign aid. One side of the debate says that not only does culture matter, but that changes in culture are needed and should be proactively sought if "Western-style" economic development is to take place in Africa and elsewhere. One African social scientist has an article and book with the title "Is Africa in Need of a Cultural Adjustment Program?" in an attempt to draw a conscious parallel with the economic change programs (some would call them "economic shock treatment programs") implemented by many African countries in the 1980s and 1990s under the close tutelage of the World Bank and IMF.[11]

The other side of the debate would also argue that culture matters, but that there are multiple cultural paths that could support economic progress and there are multiple definitions of what economic progress means. That side clearly would not favor conscious attempts to mold culture one way or another as a means of achieving economic development. It would undoubtedly argue for more home-grown, participatory models for economic development.

It is telling how closely the policy prescriptions arising from the cultural developmentalist side of the debate mirror the predominant views among donors and how the policy prescriptions of the cultural pluralists mirror the predominant views among African governments. While there are exceptions on both sides, this is largely the case even among those donors or government officials who tend not to dwell on culture as an important obstacle in the relationship or in achieving economic progress. But somehow their worldviews and economic policy preferences closely align with each of the two schools.

Despite the differing perspectives, it seems clear that whichever school you belong to, culture does matter and colors your perspective on economic development. In the next section, we will look at how some of the major cultural differences between donor nations and African countries play out in the aid setting and affect mutual understanding and trust. Before doing that, some notes of caution need to be interjected.

In a nutshell, regardless of culture's importance and who is intrinsically correct in the academic debate, attempting to manipulate culture is a dangerous and most likely hapless endeavor. Why? Because each culture is riddled with contradictions and extremes. There's also a tendency to overgeneralize and stereotype when trying to "define" culture, and it's difficult to draw the line between individual traits and cultural characteristics. Furthermore, it's impossible to ignore one's own perspective while analyzing that of another. There is always a filter when we look at other cultures. In its extreme form, that filter engenders ethnocentricity and it becomes difficult to see any culture or cultural characteristics as being superior to one's own. Another issue is that when faced with something different, people tend to seek similarities in an effort to reduce uncertainty. In other words, there may be a natural tendency to underplay cultural differences. And finally, culture is never uniform and never static. Ironically, it's both "in your face" and elusive at the same time.

Even if it were possible to sufficiently understand another culture without gross distortions, and even if—and this is a big if—the cultural developmentalists are correct about the causal link between culture and economic progress, how exactly would one go about changing culture? How do you decide which traits to leave alone ("trait-taking") and which to change ("trait-making")? To think that it's perfectly all right to pick and choose those cultural traits deemed as desirable from one particular standard is skating on pretty thin ice. And who chooses that standard and what is that standard? Efficiency? Justice? Equality? And what do you do when changes would have a differential impact on different cultural or social groups? These questions are valid even if it's your own culture, let alone someone else's.[12]

If all of the above makes you slightly uncomfortable, you're not alone. As Nathan Glazer has said: "We prefer not to refer to or make use of it today, but there does seem to be a link between race and culture, perhaps only accidental. The great races on the whole are marked by different cultures, and this connection between culture and race is one reason for our discomfort with cultural explanations."[13] And there should be even more discomfort with the notion of using deliberate cultural change as a means to another end. Just as with race, what lies beneath is either an implicit or explicit judgment that there's something inferior about that culture that needs changing.

## CULTURE AS A TOOL FOR ECONOMIC DEVELOPMENT

Can culture be used at all as a tool in economic development and in the relationship between donors and African governments? I believe that it can. By surfacing and recognizing different perspectives, many of them with deep cultural roots, it may be possible to minimize some of the existing tensions in the relationship itself. Assuming that cultural differences don't exist or aren't important has not helped the relationship. Making cultural differences more explicit may actually promote trust and mutual respect in the relationship. Once that is done, it may be possible to move on and jointly support economic development programs that build on, or are at least compatible with, African cultural traditions, instead of trying to supplant them entirely with Western notions and concepts.

It is with that perspective in mind that we now come to the point of looking at some of the major cultural differences that seem apparent between African and Western countries, and how these play out in the aid setting. There are a couple of important caveats. All of the cautions with respect to the elusive nature of culture—your own as well as that of another—apply here. I am aware that this is dangerous territory and want to reiterate that by pointing out cultural differences in a "broad brush" fashion, my intent is not to argue for or promote a certain set of cultural changes. Moreover, culture is dynamic—rapid change is happening all over the African continent, and with it, culture is also changing, although perhaps at a somewhat slower pace. Also, because of their differing origins, colonial experiences and contacts with Europeans and North Americans, Africans have diverse sets of values, ideas, and worldviews, even within the same country. Many African elites have lived and studied abroad for years. As one European ambassador posted to an African country said to me: "Culture is not a terribly great problem in my discussions. With the top level, you feel as if you are speaking with Europeans."

## CULTURAL VALUE DIFFERENCES

Despite the caveats and risk of overgeneralization, the role of cultural differences in the aid relationship is too important to ignore. There are literally dozens, if not hundreds, of ways to classify and analyze these cultural differences. The discussion below employs a fairly straightforward classification developed by Geert Hofstede about twenty-five years ago. Through empirical analysis, he derived four dimensions of cultural value differences—individualism versus collectivism; power distance; uncertainty avoidance; and masculinity-femininity.[14] We will define and look at each of these, and then look at a few specific cultural topics particularly relevant to or apparent in the aid relationship. The intention here is not to be comprehensive, but to draw attention to some of the key differences and how they seem to influence the aid relationship.

### Individualism versus Collectivism

In the West (for want of a better term), the individual and his or her goals are emphasized. Attention to individual rights, as well as the possibility or necessity for individual actions are deeply rooted beliefs in many donor countries. While there are some variations and perhaps even exceptions to this among donor countries, especially Japan and the Scandinavian countries, the dominant trend in the aid dialog undoubtedly emphasizes the need to promote and protect individual accomplishments and rights. Both market-based economic systems and democratic political systems have at their core the individual as the basic actor. As John F. Kennedy's famous quote ("Ask not what your country can do for you; ask what you can do for your country") implies, there's a belief that individuals can make all the difference. In most Western societies and organizations, individual rights and individual rewards and wealth are basic societal norms that must be reinforced and protected.

How does this play out in the aid setting? First, it is deeply embedded in the policies that are promoted with aid. There is an emphasis on promoting the rule of law, with specifics such as establishing secure individual property rights, protecting basic human rights and freedoms, and providing dependable and transparent investment and commercial "rules of the game" to encourage individual investments and wealth accumulation.

On a procedural level, the emphasis on individual responsibility is also clear. Most donors see having a sympathetic finance minister or head of state as a key ingredient to successful economic or political reform. There is faith that one person can make a difference, that individuals can break deadlocks, innovate, and create change. And when things don't go right, there is a tendency to blame and even scapegoat individuals. In practice, donors regularly, albeit usually privately, call for the removal of individuals they see as corrupt or ineffective.

This view of individual action and responsibility contrasts sharply with deeply embedded African values. The family and the community are the basic unit, not the individual. Interaction and collective gain are valued over individual autonomy and rewards. These attitudes permeate the culture, including child-rearing practices. While Western cultures encourage individualism, autonomy, and self-reliance in children, African parents are more likely to emphasize interaction, cooperation, and interdependence.[15] In addition, responsibility is more of a group concept. Referring to traditional culture in Zambia, one African author notes:

> As a collectivist society the individual did not exist as understood in the western world. What really mattered was the community in which the individual was a member. Individual responsibility was weakened by the belief that the causes of one's behaviours lay outside the individual. . . . In reporting one's mistakes, there was always a distancing of the actor from the act itself, e.g. "The axe has been broken." It is quite rare even in present time Zambia to hear reports like 'I have broken the axe! . . . Another cultural belief that discourages individual responsibility is the belief that "Man does not sin alone."[16]

Another African author reports that the belief in the overriding community interest and its accompanying egalitarianism can have the effect, sometimes aided by witchcraft, of dampening individual initiative and entrepreneurship:

> [I]nitiative and dynamism are condemned as signs of personal enrichment. The sorcerer wants equality in misery. There are numerous cases in which someone who has built a house has been told not to reside in it; others who have begun construction have been told to stop the work if they value their lives.[17]

It's fairly easy to see how this set of beliefs contrasts with those held by donors. Many governments remain skeptical of market-based policies where decisions are left up to individual buyers and sellers. Even where governments have adopted market-based policies, there is concern about how equity is affected by the policies. There is suspicion, if not outright rejection, of the "survival of the fittest" mentality that goes hand-in-hand with the notion of a competitive marketplace. In the debates over governance, individual rights, including the rights of free speech and free assembly, at times take a backseat to what is judged to be the "collective good," particularly if these freedoms carry the risk of provoking conflict and disunity within the society. While most governments are beginning to adopt Western-style legal reforms and trying to rely more heavily on the rule of law, there is still a great deal of attention paid to the unwritten traditional norms that place greater emphasis on the individual's contribution to the community.

As with the donors, these values are reflected not only in substance, but in process as well. If a minister is viewed by his or her colleagues as getting too well-known, popular, or successful as an individual, chances are that he or she will be moved out of the limelight, or at the very least be given a sound rebuke. When donors single out particular ministers or senior government officials as more helpful or easier to deal with, they may actually be doing a disservice to those officials.

Moreover, most African governments are concerned with the notion of "speaking with one voice." Several years ago in one country where I worked, the World Bank and the government agreed to hold an all-day brainstorming session between ministers and World Bank team leaders to discuss priorities for the Bank's lending. It was a lively and entertaining day, with each minister speaking his or her mind and with frank exchanges among ministers. Although not always agreeing or happy with what we heard, my World Bank colleagues were delighted with the openness of the discussion and the freedom with which senior officials presented their individual views and argued with their colleagues. However, the minister of finance who chaired the meeting was so upset with what he viewed as the frivolity and lack of discipline from his colleagues that he abruptly ended the meeting. And a couple of years later, when I proposed to the president of that country that we hold a similar meeting, it was clear that he knew all about the previous meeting and that it had stuck in his mind. He agreed to the meeting, but informed me that this time there would be "no chaos" and the government would be adequately prepared with a common position before meeting with the World Bank team. "Speaking with one voice" is also part of a bureaucracy's classic functions and culture, so it is not surprising that donor agencies share this preoccupation with their African colleagues. In this instance, cultural values concerning the collective good on the one hand, and clarity and efficiency on the other, combine to thwart real debate and dialog between governments and donors.

Corruption may be another example of how cultural differences between individually- and collectively-centered societies are playing out in the aid relationship. Corruption is an increasingly important topic in the aid dialog. Donors see it mainly as a problem of individuals and push for more laws, independent investigations, and individual prosecutions. African governments, while not denying corruption exists, are reluctant to single out and prosecute individuals. They tend to see corruption as the direct result of collective problems, for example, widespread poverty and weak institutions. Donors see the governments as not caring and not pro-active when it comes to corruption, while the governments think that the donors don't really understand the problem and are mistaking the symptoms for the disease. The result is mutual frustration. Recently, in some countries, a way forward has been found by unwittingly blending these cultural perspectives. Incumbent governments have become more willing to prosecute prominent individuals associated with previous regimes. These former government officials are unfailingly portrayed as "outsiders"—distanced from the current government—who betrayed the country and undermined the collective good for strictly individual gain.

## Power Distance

Another cultural value difference is power distance. High power-distance cultures have a strict social hierarchy, where inequality is accepted with everyone having a "rightful place" not subject to easy change. Superiors in the hierarchy have special privileges and powers denied to subordinates. In low power-distance cultures, hierarchies exist, but they are for convenience only and subordinates and superiors are considered to be the same kind of people and may change places. People in positions of power try to minimize the visible differences between themselves and their subordinates.

I once worked in an African country where a senior official directly below the minister was clearly obstructing the progress of a number of aid-supported programs. At times, he seemed to be acting with absolute impunity directly contrary to the wishes of the minister involved and the minister of finance. When I commented on this to other senior officials, one of them finally said, "Phyllis, you still don't really understand us. In our culture, he's a chief, with a much higher standing that that of either minister. No one's going to defy the chief." There was an absolute respect for hierarchy. I had merely mistaken the recently imported Western model of hierarchy for the real thing.

At the same time, there is no question that hierarchies are carefully observed and respected in the governments of African countries. Ministers are expected to have all the trappings of power—fancy cars, large offices, frequent trips abroad. What donors view as frivolous spending, the governments view as necessary symbols to signal the appropriate measure of deference and respect. Questioning authority is not common. In working-level meetings between African government teams and donor teams, it is not unusual for all donor team members to speak up and participate in the discussion. On the other hand, African officials rarely speak unless invited to do so by the most senior official present. One donor representative I interviewed had this to say:

> "We think we have effectively communicated in a meeting, but our government colleagues shouldn't always be in a listening mode. We need to have more inter-action. There are . . . problems related to hierarchy. A ministry official thinks to himself 'Only my boss can say this,' so the ministry official doesn't say anything, and his concern gets buried. The boss, meanwhile, is unsure about the implica-tions of what we are saying and what the reactions of the politicians, his bosses, will be, so he doesn't say anything either. They want to tell us, but they don't."

And when a donor mistakes all this silence for agreement, or worse, attributes the silence to not having an opinion, the possibilities for problems in the re-lationship and ineffectiveness of aid-financed programs are high.

How people view authority and hierarchy obviously has major implications for how politics are conducted and how well democratic systems function. For example, consider the idea of a "loyal opposition" so firmly entrenched in Western democratic systems. An African minister had this to say when I asked him about cultural differences:

> "On culture and belief systems, there are a lot of things taken for granted. For example, in the West, the concept of opposition is taken for granted. Here, the opposition is the enemy and there is no notion of tolerating opposition."

Ngulube provides an explanation:

> "Only one individual could be a chief at any given time or period. This means that legitimacy was personalized. . . . This personalization of office created a kind of loyalty that was first and foremost to the person and not the office. In terms of individual freedom to criticize, it was virtually unthinkable because the symbiosis between the person and the office was unbreakable. One could not criticize the person holding office without being construed to criticize the office itself."[18]

In the words of one European ambassador posted to a southern African country, "The Africans don't separate so much the person from the dossier." A senior government official was even more direct: "In our culture, heated pro-fessional arguments can't be separated from anger; we take it personally."

A colleague told me a story that illustrates this perfectly. One of his Southern African colleagues was traveling in the United States on an educational program during the "Saturday night massacre" when then President Nixon had to fire his attorney general and deputy attorney general before he could find someone to fire Archibald Cox, the Watergate special prosecutor. The Southern African official watched the commentary on television and heard the violent, hostile rhetoric from all sides. He said at the time he was convinced that the people who had disobeyed the president would be instantly taken out and shot. When my colleague met this same official some six or seven years later, he was still profoundly in awe of the American system, and amazed that President Nixon's critics had not only lived, but had lived on criticizing him.

Contrast all of the above with the culture and deeply held beliefs in Western Europe and North America involving equality, widespread participation, freedom of speech, and the absolute need for political debate and opposition. This is particularly true of the culture in the United States, which plays an important role in shaping the overall donor culture. The participatory style of most Western donors actually confounds some African officials. If everyone is speaking, who is really in charge and whom do you believe? Many African officials resent having to meet, and worse still, be lectured by what they view as "junior officials."

Some donors acknowledge that their informal, casual styles offend their African colleagues. As one northern European donor representative said to me: "For us, culture is so often a barrier . . . the way we speak, the way we dress, and we don't have much protocol. We are considered to be very brusque." In the World Bank, during one of the many reorganizations and belt-tightening exercises, all managers' offices were made smaller. After the change, several African officials worried that I had somehow lost status and standing in the institution, and they also noticed and remarked that the office of the vice president for Africa had similarly shrunk. I reassured them that it was all part of a money-saving measure, but they still looked doubtful.

The difference in cultures is perhaps most stark when looking at political and professional debates and arguments. In Deborah Tannen's book *The Argument Culture*, she makes a strong argument that Europe and North America have, in fact, gone way overboard in their citizens' affinity for debates and arguments:

> This book is about a pervasive warlike atmosphere that makes us approach public dialog, and just about anything we need to accomplish, as if it were a fight. It

is a tendency in Western culture in general, and in the United States in particular, that has a long history and a deep, thick, and far-ranging root system. It has served us well in many ways but in recent years has become so exaggerated that it is getting in the way of solving our problems. Our spirits are corroded by living in an atmosphere of unrelenting contention—an argument culture.[19]

Behind the notion of the "argument culture" that Tannen describes is a profound belief in the equality of the parties and the fluidity of society and decision making. If you make your case often enough and loudly enough, you have the possibility of prevailing. In societies where hierarchies are rigid, these types of arguments are unacceptable. It is positively "cheeky" to argue with the chief, whoever the chief may be. Moreover, it does no good. Decisions are not made by debate among all levels of the hierarchy; decisions are made at the top.

Imagine how this plays out in the aid and development dialog. Donors, schooled in a culture of open debate, expect African government officials to engage in lively policy debates with them. In contrast, these same officials equate money with power and assume that the decisions have already been made elsewhere. Arguing is useless, and even worse, their opposition could be taken personally and make the powerful donors angry. Too often, the result is silence, a silence that donors, particularly those with less experience, can easily mistake for acquiescence. Alternatively, when confronted with strong positions and strong arguments, senior government officials may simply "dig in their heels" and say no—end of discussion. This wins them the reputation of being uncooperative or obstructionist. Either way, the damage to the aid relationship and aid effectiveness is palpable.

> Whatever the causes of the argument culture . . . the most grievous cost is the **price paid in human spirit:** Contentious public discourse becomes a model for behavior and sets the tone for how individuals experience their relationships to other people and to the society we live in.[20]

The obvious alternative is a process of dialog and consensus-building, of looking painstakingly for common ground and underlying interests, instead of emphasizing differences and rigid positions. Theoretically, this approach is compatible across cultures and has been recognized in Western management theory as a successful path in negotiations.[21] But as we will see later on, cultural preoccupations with time and the pressures on and within aid bureaucracies and African governments provide powerful roadblocks to this approach.

## Uncertainty Avoidance

Another important dimension of cultural difference is uncertainty avoidance, the extent to which a culture feels threatened by uncertainty and ambiguity. In cultures with high uncertainty avoidance, there is prevailing anxiety and uncertainty and an accompanying tendency to fight these with formal rule systems, a belief in expert knowledge, and a low tolerance for dissent. In contrast, societies with low uncertainty avoidance more easily accept uncertainty, have greater tolerance, and rely more on common sense. As with all cultural differences, no society is pure and many societies have mixed tendencies. Northern European cultures generally exhibit more tolerance and less fear of uncertainty; the United States is perhaps more toward the middle. While still moving along a spectrum, the various African cultures are relatively more anxious about uncertainty and less tolerant.[22] In the poorer African countries, precarious economic conditions only serve to heighten insecurity.

When you feel like you are already "living on the edge" and life is difficult and constantly fraught with uncertainties, it becomes difficult to take risks and deviate from established patterns. Even leaving aside long-standing cultural dimensions, the continual changes in Africa over the last thirty-five years—because of independence, wars, drought, floods, coups, AIDS—are enough to make anyone's head spin. When the government changes, everything can change. The economic and political systems are transformed. Relatives associated with the previous regime lose their jobs and sometimes, even their lives. There is little to depend on, except the comfort of the extended family or village and the traditional rules that change only very slowly.

Contrast this with Western Europe or the United States. While these societies are now also subject to technology-induced rapid change, changes in everyday life are slow and seem barely noticeable. Elections come and go, with little discernible impact on the majority of the voting public. After the 2000 presidential election in the United States, for more than one month it was uncertain who the president would be. And what happened? Absolutely nothing, except for an outpouring of commentaries from news analysts and a stream of jokes from late-night comedians. People went about their business, secure in the knowledge that whatever the result, life would continue much as before.

How does uncertainty avoidance affect the aid dialog? First, attitudes toward change are very different among donors and African governments. In the donor countries, change and innovation are encouraged; change is almost always presumed to be for the better. So the donors' natural prescription for African countries is change, the faster the better. Not surprisingly, many African countries are resistant to change. Cultural norms, as well as recent events, reinforce the fact that change is not necessarily a good thing. Furthermore, even if enormous change efforts are undertaken, experience teaches that it can all be wiped away in a minute, by either natural or man-made catastrophes, so deliberate change is approached cautiously, if at all. The experimentation and innovation embraced by the donors are viewed as reckless adventures by their African counterparts.

There have been, of course, fundamental changes undertaken by African governments over the last thirty years or so. Among many donors, a prevailing view is that these are "too little, too late" or are merely commonplace and common sense. Viewed from a different cultural prism, the deliberate changes that have occurred are true acts of courage undertaken against tremendous odds. Many African leaders resent donors for underestimating their achievements.

Cultural differences also magnify the disappointments that have accompanied development policy and program failures. At least in the beginning, African governments were prepared to yield to the advice of "experts" brought in from other countries. In cultures where there is low tolerance for uncertainty, there is a strong faith in the specialist—be it a witch doctor or a development specialist—who has the right answer. They believed what they were told—if an African country followed the magic formulas of Western economists, prosperity would ensue. So many African governments accepted without question the advice of the experts and followed the policy prescriptions and project plans.

Even without engaging in the long debate as to whether the formulas actually work or whether they were faithfully followed, one thing is clear: prosperity did not arrive. In the donor countries, it is taken for granted that a so-called expert is far from infallible and that not everything will go according to plan. But there is a strong culture of "nothing ventured, nothing gained" and "try, try again." In contrast, African governments expected more certainty and more success from experts, and the disillusion has been intense.

In many African countries, there is now a feeling that they let themselves become willing victims through an undue reliance on the power of outside experts. In turn, the experts acknowledge some failures on their part, but mostly blame failure on faulty implementation by the Africans. In any event, the result is mistrust in the relationship and a marked reluctance to rely on outside advice.

In a world fraught with anxiety and uncertainty, rigid rules and predictable outcomes are highly prized. And in that context, donor predictability and reliability are a big deal. Yet, as we will see in the next chapter, there are a number of external and internal pressures on aid bureaucracies that undermine their ability to deliver. In more flexible and certain environments, changes and delays—such as those that normally occur in aid programs—are seen mostly as temporary setbacks and are taken for granted and absorbed in some fashion. In Africa, where uncertainty is pervasive, each and every change or delay feels like a body blow—and can and does have dire economic consequences in the precarious circumstances that characterize many African economies. Promises by donors become just one more unpredictable feature of life—not to be taken seriously and not to be counted on.

Differing cultural views toward uncertainty emerge most sharply in the debate over governance. Both donor nations and African governments place a lot of emphasis on rule of law. The question is really which law and what kind of law. Part of the democratic ideal is respect and tolerance for minorities and dissenting voices. Dissent in Western Europe and North America is viewed as strengthening the political system, not endangering it. The high levels of uncertainty, anxiety, and instability make tolerance a difficult concept in Africa. As discussed before, dissent is viewed as disrespect. Indeed, one needs only to look at almost any opposition newspaper in Africa to see frequent attempts to not only question policy, but to assassinate character, with liberal interpretation of "facts." In turn, official newspapers make what they consider to be justified 'preemptive strikes' or attack back in a similar vein. Underlying the lack of tolerance is fear. There is no guarantee that dissenters will play by the rules, and in many African countries, dissent has spiraled into conflict and chaos. Viewed from an African perspective, tolerance is at best a double-edged sword in a fragile and uncertain political and economic environment.

On a more abstract level, the underlying principles governing both market economics and multiparty democracy are based on embracing uncertainty.

Both have elements of a contest—outcomes are not predetermined, and "let the best man win." In a world where uncertainty is feared, these systems seem to bring greater uncertainty, not less. It is perhaps not surprising that socialism, with its five-year plans, quotas, and strong central governments, found such fertile ground in Africa. It didn't leave much room for individual initiative, and at least in theory, for the unexpected. It is also not much of a surprise that corruption is an issue throughout most of Africa. When you don't know what tomorrow will bring, grabbing what you can, when you can, makes sense. Having faith in tomorrow and building for the future are luxuries in an uncertain world.

### Masculinity/Femininity

A fourth dimension of cultural variability developed by Hofstede is masculinity/femininity. As defined by him, masculinity is associated with assertiveness, an emphasis on money and material possessions, and unequal sex roles, with women relegated to the relatively unimportant task of nurturing. In contrast, feminine-oriented cultures place more emphasis on the quality of life, nurturing and relationships, and equal roles for the sexes.

As with each of the cultural variables, it is difficult to generalize. While the United States can be recognized as a masculine culture, the Scandinavian countries are less so. In Africa, women have occupied important roles as the main economic providers in families, and there are numerous examples of women as chiefs. There is, however, also marked inequality in access by women to schooling and positions of power within African governments. At the same time, African cultures place relatively more emphasis on quality of life and relationships as opposed to material wealth alone. On a continuum with masculinity on one end and femininity on the other, Africa tends toward the feminine side.

The implications for the aid relationship are perhaps obvious. Market-based economic systems are all about the creation of individual wealth. Traditionally, in African societies, there is a suspicion and jealousy of those who are wealthier than the surrounding community. There is a presumption of a zero-sum game—more wealth for him necessarily means less wealth for me. Moreover, material possessions are far less important than one's position within the family and community, as well as the maintenance of those ties and other traditional values. Africans tend to view Western societies as cold places where only money counts. While there is no question that Africans want a better life and relief from human suffering, their definition of a better life is not limited to having more money. And they are suspicious of an economic system that places its entire emphasis on getting more money. As elsewhere in this chapter, some caution on overgeneralization is needed here: Western culture produced Mother Teresa, while Zaire's Mobutu spent a lifetime amassing personal wealth. Neither though can be considered typical of their respective cultures.

In addition to skepticism about "the magic of the marketplace," these attitudes toward material wealth directly influence the aid relationship. Donors tend to see aid mostly in terms of a business transaction. Money is given in exchange for reforms or carrying out specific development programs in specific ways. Money is viewed—and used—as a powerful incentive to make things happen. For Africans, aid is seldom seen as a straightforward business transaction. Relatively minor changes or delays disrupt fragile plans and color the way Africans see "the deal." More importantly, money is not seen as the only or even the most important ingredient in the aid relationship. The constant refrain in this book is precisely that it is not the money alone that counts. The money, while absolutely necessary, carries a symbolic significance that is not always fully appreciated by the donors. Aid is money, but it is also a symbol of confidence, friendship, and that all-important word—trust. And if money means that you will be perceived as relinquishing your sovereignty or tarnishing your image as a leader, it simply isn't worth it. The distance between Wall Street and Cairo Road (the main street in downtown Lusaka) cannot be measured in miles alone.

Differing cultural attitudes toward assertiveness also come into play. Western cultures expect people to vigorously defend their points of view. Power and assertiveness go hand in hand. As mentioned previously, Western cultures can increasingly be characterized as "argument cultures." In Africa, assertiveness is generally identified with individualism, rebellion, and disrespect. Being assertive is, more often than not, viewed as being out of control—either of one's emotions or the situation. More importantly, it is not necessarily associated with power. As one manifestation, many African leaders are soft-spoken. In meetings, subordinates and visitors have to lean in, listening intently to try and capture what it is being said. In Africa, that is a true picture of power—people hanging on your every word, even if spoken barely above a whisper.

This cultural attitude toward assertiveness at times exasperates the donors. I have sat through countless meetings with governments where various segments of civil society or donors attack government policies or priorities. In most cases, the attacks are left uncontested or even unanswered by government officials who are present. One is left with the impression of a government unable or unwilling to defend its own policies, or even worse, of a government that feels no ownership over what it is doing. While surely there are instances where one of those is the case, the government's stance is usually rooted in a differing cultural perspective. The leader does not defend decisions. He explains decisions at a time and place of his own choosing. A vigorous defense and a public argument are culturally not acceptable, and may be interpreted as a sign of weakness and ebbing power.

The same sort of dynamic plays out in private meetings. In my own meetings with heads of state and other senior officials, as well as the numerous accounts I have had of such meetings involving other donors, silence and soft words are prominent features, at least on the African side. Too often I have heard stories along this vein:

> "I went to see him, and we exchanged pleasantries. When I spoke of our issues and problems, he said very little. When I stopped speaking, he thanked me for my visit and I was ushered out. I was very frank and critical, but I am not even sure he heard what I was saying. I got so frustrated I repeated myself, and I found myself growing annoyed. He gave no sign that he had heard or understood. Frankly, I doubt it."

The idea that a head of state or other senior official would grant a senior aid representative an audience and then *not* hear or listen to what was said is implausible at best. What is at work here are different cultural styles and norms. The more senior the leader, the less likely he or she is to engage in spirited debate. That does not mean that he has not listened or that he does not have strong views. Particularly in such formal settings, debate and defense are viewed as highly inappropriate. In contrast, most of the donors expect, at the very least, a show of understanding and a reasoned defense of government policy. Too often, the result of such a meeting is that the diplomat or aid official is left with the impression of an uninformed or unengaged leader. In turn, the African official is left with the impression of a rude and arrogant diplomat.

I am leaving this section with silence on unequal sex roles. While gender issues are important topics in both Africa and the donor nations, I did not witness a cultural divide or big differences on this topic that influence the aid relationship. Gender discrimination in professional and personal life, as well as a few examples of extraordinary women in senior positions, are the general picture in both aid bureaucracies and African governments. In the society at large, of course, the differences are more substantial. Inadequate legal protection for women in many countries, coupled with some traditional values and practices, have left African women highly vulnerable to extreme poverty and AIDS.

## COMMUNICATION STYLES, CONCEPTS OF TIME, AND EDUCATION EXPERIENCES

In addition to the broad dimensions of cultural variability described above, there are numerous other specific cultural differences. Different religious traditions, concepts of family, the degree of formality, and the use of space are just examples. In the interviews I conducted, the three mentioned most frequently as having an impact on the aid relationship were communication styles, concepts of time, and education.

### Communication

A number of culturally rooted communication differences have already been mentioned, but there are others. The noted anthropologist Edward Hall makes the distinction between high-context and low-context communication.[23] In high-context communication, the meaning of what is communicated is not so much in the words or the message itself, but is embodied in the setting and the people who are sending and receiving the message. In contrast, low-context communication relies much more on the explicit message itself. As Hall points out, no culture is exclusively high-context or low-context, but cultures fall along a spectrum. The United States and European nations tend to have cultures and communication styles that are low-context. As my precocious three-year-old nephew once said when queried about the meaning of the sentences he had just rattled off out loud from *Time Magazine*, "What do you mean 'what does it mean?' It means what it says." In contrast, Africa and Asia are generally on the higher end of the context scale. The meaning of any message is highly influenced by who's talking, who's listening, and the particular situation.

How does this difference affect the aid relationship? In the words of one donor representative, "The officials in this country are highly sensitive to form and nuance. They come away with three options about how to interpret everything they hear from us." In other words, the words are not so important, and meaning is highly dependent on context. Room for confusion and misinterpretation is ample, more so now that the aid business has become so intricately linked with diplomacy. Diplomacy has its own language, one that is more high-context than that normally used by nondiplomatic donor representatives. But in an environment where African governments have to contend with both diplomats and non-diplomats from the same countries, confusion is perhaps inevitable. For example, there are numerous examples where both sides come away from high-level meetings with completely different impressions.

One case with which I am familiar was a meeting between senior African officials and a senior European diplomat in circumstances where relations between the two countries could best be described as fragile. The Africans thought the meeting had gone quite well and looked forward to an increase in aid. Used to the more explicit language of aid bureaucrats, they thought the mild tone and general language in the meeting signaled that the diplomat had understood their country's difficulties and was prepared to help. In fact, the European interpretation of the meeting was quite different, and aid was further cut back.

To try and counteract some of the confusion and misunderstandings that arise in aid discussions, donor representatives at times become even more explicit about what they mean, explaining everything in great detail. Overexplaining also happens when international development specialists don't have the time to become familiar with a particular country's circumstances. This, in turn, can and is easily interpreted by government officials as donors "talking down" to them. Hall points out a similar phenomenon with management consultants:

> Modern management methods, for which management consultants are largely responsible, are less successful than they should be, because in an attempt to make everything explicit (low-contexting again) they frequently fail in their recommendations to take into account what people already know. This is a common fault of the consultant, because few consultants take the time (and few

clients will pay for the time) to become completely contexted in the many complexities of the business.[24]

The difference between low-context and high-context communication cultures may also explain why several government officials mentioned to me their preference for verbal communication. Two ministers had this to say:

"We have an oral tradition. What matters more is what's said rather than what's written. If someone sends me a letter, but doesn't talk to me about it, I tend to ignore it."

"There is too much written communication based on incomplete discussion."

For those of us who come from low-context cultures, it is hard to understand that a conversation can mean more than a written communication where everything is laid down in black and white. In fact, those of us in the aid business are forever urging our staffs to put everything down in aid memoirs and letters. But in high-context cultures, nothing is ever black and white, and the context is all important. A conversation provides much more context than a letter.

Communication, of course, also has a physical dimension. Here, too, there are cultural differences. The best example is eye contact. As one senior government official succinctly explained:

"There are a lot of cultural misunderstandings. For example, in our culture, I wouldn't look you straight in the eye; in your culture, this would mean I have something to hide."

A second area is protocol—seating, attendance at meetings, dress, and a host of other physical issues. Although there are exceptions, official Africa is formal, much more so than the United States and northern Europe. Some aid representatives, either wittingly or unwittingly, behave in a more informal manner, in hopes perhaps of encouraging a more open and frank exchange. More often than not, it is interpreted as a sign of disrespect.

### Concepts of Time

Differing concepts of time provide major irritants in the aid relationship. Let's start with an anecdote. A European ambassador to an African country told me the story of one of his colleagues. It is customary that at official events, the diplomatic corps is asked to arrive early and to take seats to await the head of state of the country. Once the announced time for the president's arrival came and went with no sign of the president, *every single time* this particular diplomat would point to his watch and say with irritation, "This would never happen in my country." Both the European ambassador who told me the story and the African colleagues to whom I told the story had the same reaction: "You would think that after three years in the country, this guy would have figured out that the president never arrives at the appointed time," followed by some words to the effect that he needed to "chill out."

It's easy to laugh at the punctual diplomat, but it's not so funny when you travel thirty hours straight only to find that no one is available to receive you at your confirmed appointment or when a tight schedule becomes shredded because each and every meeting gets delayed, cancelled, or rescheduled. There are numerous examples of seminars in African countries that involve people flying in from different countries that are called off at the last minute "because the minister has to travel." Similarly, African officials don't find it amusing at all when their country is denied millions of dollars of aid just because they miss a deadline by a few days or when they are asked to circumvent their own legal procedures just to get something done "on time."

People from donor countries generally tend to associate punctuality with courtesy and respect. Similarly, respect for deadlines is associated with commitment, "seriousness," and efficiency. On the other side, African officials tend to view aid officials as "slaves to the clock" who forget that life is complicated and that juggling is inevitable. Having a deadline merely for the sake of having a deadline is mechanistic and artificial. It is also a sign of disrespect, since a deadline implies theirs is the only or most important thing that needs to be done, regardless of what else is going on.

Edward Hall has written specifically on the cultural dimensions of time, and has concluded that complex societies organize time in at least two different ways. Cultures working with monochronic time (M-time) schedule events as separate items one at a time. Tasks, schedules, and procedures are important. In contrast, cultures that work with polychronic time (P-time) are involved in several things at once. For cultures on P-time, the involvement of people is what matters rather than preset schedules. Time is seldom considered to be wasted; if you value people, you can't cut them off in mid-sentence.[25]

Most donor countries are on M-time, while African countries are on P-time. As Hall points out, neither one is intrinsically better. M-time compartmentalizes things and cuts people off from the larger context; it is often blind to the needs of people. P-time recognizes complexities of life and people, but is often dependent on the abilities of a central figure to stay on top of things and handle emergencies.

Both concepts of time may be of intrinsic worth, but there is no question that M-timers and P-timers annoy each other. It is difficult to underestimate the importance that differing concepts of time have in the aid relationship. The core elements that are critical to the relationship and to the establishment of trust—shared purposes, commitment, and reliability—are in one way or another bound up with notions of time. With the advent of the electronic information era and the concept of "multitasking," there is a growing realization in M-time societies of a different approach to time that resembles P-time in some aspects. Similarly, because many African officials have studied abroad in M-time societies, there is an understanding of some of the advantages of M-time. Nonetheless, there is still the image of an Africa "where nothing gets done," accompanied by relentless efforts by donors to guide the relationship through a plethora of tight schedules and deadlines. This is symptomatic of a relationship where M-time is the dominant concept of time, one viewed as indispensable to successful aid programs and development.

### Education

No chapter on culture would be complete without reference to education. Education, along with family and community, is one of the great transmitters of cultural norms. The educational systems in both donor and African nations reinforce the differing cultural perspectives we have discussed and thus affect the aid relationship. This is not the place for a detailed discussion of the different educational systems and their effects. But there is one important aspect of Africa's educational systems as inherited from the colonial powers that warrants explicit mention. In the words of one African official:

> "When I left to study abroad, I had to learn how to listen and how to think. In our system, this was not taught . . . the educational system inherited from the British was designed to train subordinates. The system hasn't changed much and people are still scared to make decisions."

This contrasts sharply, at least in theory, with the type of education offered in donor nations and particularly in the United States. In those systems, the whole point is not to learn by rote, but to learn to learn. Initiative and problem solving are at the heart of the system. Without intending to blame all of Africa's current problems on its colonial past, it is clear that some of the colonial legacies, like the educational system, have affected how African bureaucracies are organized, how they work, and how their officials relate to their colleagues from the donor agencies.

This chapter has tried to show how some of the cultural differences between donor countries and African nations affect the aid relationship. It is by no means exhaustive, and has focused on those aspects of culture that have an evident effect on the aid relationship. Necessarily, it has had to rely on generalizations, but the topic is simply too important to ignore. One of the goals has been to try and convince skeptics, including the many technical specialists working in donor agencies, that culture matters and matters deeply in aid relationships, and therefore in development effectiveness. In closing this chapter, I want to reiterate that understanding the profound effects of culture does not provide a license to manipulate it or attempt to induce cultural change from the outside. Nathan Glazer provides an appropriate summation:

> I think culture does make a difference. But it is hard to determine what in culture makes the difference. . . . [The great cultural traditions] have all had their glories and their miseries, their massacres and their acts of charity, their scholars and their soldiers, their triumphs of intellectual achievement and their descents into silliness or worse. Rather, it makes more sense to think of them as storehouses from which practices suitable for and useful for all may emerge.[26]

Viewing Africa's cultural traditions as a storehouse rather than an obstacle may be a useful place to begin.

## NOTES

1. Glazer 2000, p. 220.

2. Samovar and Porter 1991a, p. 50.

3. Fukuyama 1996, p. 34.

4. Shweder 2000, p. 163.

5. Samovar and Porter 1991a, p. 51.

6. Fukuyama 1996, p. 33.

7. Inglehart 2000, p. 82; Inglehart 1997; and Inglehart and Baker 2000.

8. Shweder 2000, p. 164.

9. Weisner 2000, p. 141–42

10. Weisner 2000, p. 148.

11. Etounga-Manguelle 2000, pp. 65–77.

12. These sections on both the problems of defining culture and the difficulties of using culture as a tool in economic development are based on a number of sources, including Klitgaard (1997, pp. 191–202), Samovar and Porter (1991a, especially pp. 54–63), and Glazer (2000, pp. 219–30).

13. Glazer 2000, pp. 220–21.

14. Hofstede 1980. For brief summaries of Hofstede's classifications, see also Gudykunst and Nishida 1989, especially pp. 21–22, Samovar and Porter 1991a, especially pp. 127–30, and Gudykunst and Ting-Toomey 1988, especially chapter 2, pp. 39–60.

15. Weisner 2000, p. 145

16. Ngulube 1997, pp. 114–15

17. Etounga-Manguelle 2000, p. 75. Ngulube (1997) provides a host of similar examples, especially, p. 122.

18. Ngulube 1997, p. 33.

19. Tannen 1998, p. 3

20. Tannen 1998, p. 280.

21. The classic in this regard is Fisher, Ury, and Patton 1991.

22. Ngulube 1997, pp. 139–42 and Samovar and Porter 1991a, p. 129.

23. Hall 1977.

24. Hall 1991, p. 49.

25. This section is based on Hall 1983, especially pp. 41–54.

26. Glazer, "Disaggregating Culture" in *Culture Matters*, p. 230.

# 5

# Institutional Roadblocks

In the last chapter we saw how differing cultural traditions and assumptions can affect the aid relationship and stand in the way of dialog, listening, and learning. This, in turn, undermines building trust and mutual influence, ingredients needed to reshape development efforts and improve aid effectiveness in Africa. In this chapter, we take a look at the political, institutional, and bureaucratic constraints that make it difficult for donor staff to change the way they currently operate.

There are many points in the following discussion that apply equally well to African governments. In addition, there is a host of other issues affecting African governments that is usually captured in the catchall phrase "lack of capacity." These issues can't and shouldn't be ignored, and they haven't been. Low educational levels, tangled bureaucracies, and the general disarray of most African governments have not gone unnoticed, either by academics or *The Financial Times*, *Washington Post*, or *New York Times*. But as we have seen, there are also the questions of "capacity to do what" and "capacity to do how."

Without absolving African governments for their share of responsibility in the lackluster performance of aid or in the troubled relationship with donors, it is important to focus on the donor side of the equation, which has generally received less attention. That is beginning to change. In recent years, there has been a fair amount of criticism of aid donors, on the streets and in the press, mostly in connection with the antiglobalization movement. Critics charge that most foreign aid and the policies and programs it supports only make the poor poorer and the rich richer. They accuse donors—and especially multilateral institutions such as the World Bank—of shoddy motives and shoddy programs, not to mention shoddy behavior in coercing African governments to accept what they say.

Life would be easier if it were that simple. As the discussion in the previous chapters has tried to convey, the business of foreign aid and development in Africa is complex. There are good motives and not so good motives, along with successful programs and programs that don't get off the ground. There may well be instances of coercion, but there are at least as many cultural misunderstandings. The true smoking gun lies in the absence of dialog and trust among donors and African governments so that policies and programs are faulty from the start, or don't get implemented in a manner that leads to lasting change. By talking about the numerous institutional and political hurdles that foreign aid workers face, my intention is not to feed the forces of antiglobalization. I, along with most people working in development, share the protesters' frustration and their concern for the poor. But their analysis is too simplistic and displays ignorance of the dynamics within and among developing countries and the governments and international agencies that provide aid.

The vast majority of people who get involved with development work do so because they are committed to helping people out of poverty. For many, the World Bank's slogan, "Our dream is a world free of poverty," is corny, but true. But there are a lot of obstacles to realizing that dream. Development specialists are increasingly caught in the crossfire generated by the larger factors at play in aid decisions. Added to this is a work environment that is becoming increasingly uncertain and difficult. In the next sections, we take a look at the institutional factors affecting how development agencies do their work and how this affects their relationship with the African governments.

## THE "BIG PICTURE" FACTORS

Concerns over the lack of aid effectiveness ironically have created an overall environment in which aid is made *even less effective*. Cuts in the budgets and staffing of development agencies accompanied cuts in overall aid levels in the 1990s. During the second half of the 1990s, World Bank senior management made a pact with the Bank's board of directors that is called the Strategic

Compact. In exchange for some additional budget resources for a few years, management would realign the strategic direction of the Bank and in some key areas make it more efficient. In 2000, budget levels would return to pre-Compact levels—presumably with no harm done, the Bank having become a leaner, more efficient organization.

In 2000, as promised, the operational budgets were cut back. What was the result? Not exactly what was expected—firing of staff, cancelled trips, and postponed operations, and sinking staff morale. Why? Because in the meanwhile, there were new and urgent demands placed on the Bank. These included, but were by no means limited to, taking a lead role in the fight against HIV/AIDS, especially in Africa; accelerating debt relief for the poorest nations; and helping countries to work out detailed poverty reduction strategies. These three are good examples because the Group of Seven industrialized nations, referred to as the G-7, explicitly charged the Bank to do more on each of these, and each takes considerable money and staff.[1]

At the same time, there was concern that the Bank needed to increase lending and resource transfers to developing countries. *And* there was concern that the Bank continue to pay attention to increasing the quality and development impact of its lending operations and measuring results. *And* Bank staff were expected to be more accessible and spend more time with the individuals and groups interested in their work—Congressional aides, other donors, nongovernmental organizations (NGOs), and the media. *And,* if there were new world developments, such as floods in Mozambique or reconstruction in East Timor, Afghanistan, or Iraq, Bank staff, as a matter of course, were to jump on a plane and get there fast with technical advice and financial assistance. The demands on Bank staff far outstrip the limited budgeted increases since 2000. It is testimony to the dedication of Bank staff and their belief in the "dream" that well over two-thirds reported in late 2003 that their morale at work was high.[2]

### Stretched Thin

In this scenario, where budget increases do not keep pace with the workload, the staff and managers who do the Bank's operational work are caught in the middle, stretched very thin. Because of their commitment to making a difference many staff have adjusted by working longer hours. But in one of the many catch-22s in a large bureaucracy, there is really no meaningful way to record the extra hours worked without showing a "budget overrun," despite the fact that technical staff and managers don't get paid for overtime. In essence, the Bank now runs on lots of unrecorded, and at least in some sense, uncompensated, overtime by dedicated staff. Some 45 percent of Bank staff believe that work pressures are at unacceptable levels, and over one-third reported that work pressures harmed their health over the last year.[3]

While I used a concrete example from the World Bank, this situation is by no means unique. Another donor representative had this to say: "The staff from headquarters are hassled, stressed out, and feel pushed around. They try their best within their constraints. . . . When a team comes here, it's like a train racing through. They need more time, and it stands in the way of our having a better relationship with the government." And that's really the point. For donor agency staff, taking the time to dialog, to get the facts straight and sort out issues, to listen carefully, and to change or redo plans because of what you heard, are luxuries they can't afford. Paired off with government staff who frequently are overworked, unmotivated, or ill prepared, it's easy to see why real conversations don't take place. As one senior minister told me: "Sometimes when technical experts are on short trips here, their work is superficial, and from that they draw big conclusions and recommendations. Sometimes we listen to their reports in silence because we are embarrassed for them—how much they don't know or got wrong."

Cuts in aid budgets—and even annual *increases* in aid budgets—create their own vicious cycle. Individual country "desks" compete for resources on an annual basis within most aid bureaucracies. In an overall environment where money is scarce, it is naturally frowned upon if the money allocated to a particular country for grants or loans isn't spent. It could well result in that country having a lower amount available the following year.[4] Several ambassadors and aid representatives told me that in the rush to get projects ready and make grants, staff or consultants were sent in to do things that government staff could do perfectly well, albeit more slowly, or even worse, that the projects weren't exactly what the government wanted. Several rightly worried that implementation would suffer. But at the same time, they were even more worried that if the allocation were cut, they would *never* be able to get it back again, even when it was clearly needed. Many also saw their own careers caught up in this dynamic. It's not good to become known as someone who can't even manage to give money away.

**Need to Lend**

In the 1980s and early 1990s, the World Bank was heavily criticized for having a "pressure to lend" culture that put much more emphasis on making loans than on actual implementation and results on the ground. In response to that criticism, the Bank took a series of measures to counteract that pressure. It eliminated the explicit link between the amount of lending in a country and the size of the budget available to staff working on the country. It instituted a Quality Assurance Group, randomly sampling operations both at the approval stage and during implementation, to ensure that shortcuts did not undermine quality. It advised staff that managing big lending operations was no longer the leading or sole criteria for promotion to senior levels.

While all of these changes heightened awareness and perhaps took the edge off the problem, it didn't eliminate the pressure to lend.[5] Why? Because the World Bank faces the same dilemmas that country desks face in bilateral aid agencies. For the poorest countries, mostly located in Africa, the Bank provides loans under the International Development Association (IDA). These "loans" are highly concessional, with a thirty-five- or forty-year term, a ten-year grace period, and a service charge of .75 percent. IDA receives donations from the richer countries and must be periodically replenished. There is an IDA allocation system that takes into account performance, need, and debt sustainability and sets lending limits per country. So there is not an unconstrained pressure to lend at the country level. But all staff working on IDA countries are aware that if the Bank is unable to "spend" existing IDA resources within the envisioned timetable, it will be a hard sell to convince parliaments around the world, including the U.S. Congress, to vote the needed funds for yet another replenishment. And if the World Bank can't successfully transfer available resources and get development moving in the poorest countries, this calls into question its very reason for being. It is not hard to see how, despite the existence of mostly competent and committed staff, that the rush to make new loans and grants and spend money gets in the way of capacity-building and a true dialog and partnership between donor agencies and African governments. One donor representative summed this up perfectly: "Influencing takes time. We are risking our relations by piling too much on. There is a tension between influencing and spending."

## Pressures of Politics

Aid budgets are usually decided upon by legislatures, which brings with it other pressures that get in the way of increasing trust and improving aid effectiveness.[6] The effect of politics on aid decisions was blatant during the Cold War. Although playing out in different ways, it is no less so today. For one thing, politicians have short time horizons—a year or two is a long time. Politicians who are subject to reelection every few years want quick results. Unfortunately, most development activities take a long time, and there are few quick fixes. You might be able to build a road in a year or so, but it will take a little longer to see the effect. Sometimes the effects are fairly rapid—for a farmer, the road will give him access to new markets, allow him to make changes in what he grows and to whom he sells, and maybe make more money. But in the case of the child who can now go to school more easily—and more often—the effects of the road will only be revealed years later.

So how can politicians in donor countries "sell" aid to their constituencies and show them that something is happening? One way is to finance as much "concrete" as possible. That way you can point to roads, schools, health posts, and other tangible "stuff."[7] Never mind that the road will fall apart without routine maintenance; there's no qualified teacher and an inappropriate curriculum; and there's no trained health worker or drugs. Those things take time and are more "invisible." In other words, the short-term perspective of most politicians distorts what gets financed by aid.

## Aid Fads

This anxiety for short-term results also leads directly to "aid fads" mentioned in chapter 1. Development specialists are constantly looking for new approaches, which is healthy. But the need to demonstrate quick results to the people who hold the purse strings leads to some perverse behavior. New approaches are brought in by development agencies with considerable fanfare and are heralded and imitated even before any meaningful implementation has taken place. This was certainly the case for integrated rural development projects in the 1970s and for sector investment programs in the late 1990s.[8] New approaches such as these are "sold" to both donor and recipient governments as the solutions to previous problems limiting the effectiveness of aid. When results are slow to materialize—as they inevitably are—disillusionment quickly sets in. The approach is either discarded or merely forgotten, and it's on to the next one. The approach may or may not have intrinsic merit, but the impatience for fast results robs us of the chance to find out. And this same impatience makes African governments feel railroaded every time a donor comes up with yet another "good idea," cooked up in Washington or London or Oslo, and their development specialists come charging onto the African continent.

To be fair, there are development officials who caution against this "flavor of the month" behavior and who have also convinced their politicians to turn away from financing only buildings and other infrastructure. And just because something is a fad doesn't mean it has no value. In many ways, integrated rural development projects were the intellectual precursor to the more comprehensive development approach in vogue today. And the sector investment programs have been instrumental in shifting some donors away from projects and "concrete" toward longer-term program support. We'll highlight how things are changing in the next chapter, but there is no denying that things are changing far too slowly.

### Special Interests

In addition to the limited time horizons that go hand-in-hand with political decision-making processes, there is now a multitude of special interest groups involved in development issues throughout the donor countries. These NGOs are bringing their perspectives to the table through direct lobbying and pressure on legislatures and aid agencies. Their interests are far ranging—biological diversity, debt relief, child labor laws, gender equality, human rights, closing the digital divide, multiparty democracy, HIV/AIDS prevention and treatment, religious interests, and protection of indigenous groups, to name only a few. Most of the issues are important. Some, like HIV/AIDS and debt relief, are so fundamental to Africa's future that they rightfully have moved front and center on the agenda of most African governments and donors. And these groups have played an important role in making that happen.

But the problem is that there are just too many special interests with too many demands on development agencies and African governments. Sometimes NGOs, through successful lobbying of legislatures, manage to place specific legal restrictions on the use of aid. Other times, they are able to convince aid agencies— either because of true conviction or because of fear of repercussions—to place greater emphasis on a particular issue or to start a brand new initiative.

What's wrong with this? After all, most of these are valid concerns. The problem is that one size doesn't fit all, and not every issue holds the same priority in every country. And what happens to the voices of the African governments and African people in the process? If everything is a priority, nothing is a priority. If priorities are imported from outside, the role of African governments is fundamentally diminished. As one senior African official said to me:

> "We perceive principles of democracy as being important . . . [but] the donors consulting the NGOs are creating a difficult situation. The NGOs are being taken as a proxy for democratic voices, but the truth is that they don't necessarily represent the wishes of the people. . . . NGOs should also be subject to democratic norms and standards. . . . The question becomes who did we elect: the NGOs, the donors? Why are we bothering with elections then?"

Apart from the philosophical questions, there are also practical ones. So many competing ideas and priorities create a bazaar-like atmosphere. Within this atmosphere, it's easy for development specialists to lose sight of what's really fundamental. There's also the time involved for aid officials to meet with NGOs and discuss issues with them. These meetings are useful to exchange information. NGOs, especially if they are local organizations with grassroots ties, can increase the donors' understanding of particular issues. But the time commitment is substantial and comes at the cost of other potential uses of time, including field visits. This may be a worthwhile trade-off, but it needs to be recognized that it is part of a trade-off. There are benefits, but there are also costs.

These meetings between NGOs and donors return us to a central question. More often than not, when donors meet with NGOs the government is not present. Sometimes, it's because the NGO or the donor insists on a separate relationship, and sometimes it's because the government declines the invitation. These separate meetings inevitably raise questions. Why do NGOs feel they have to work through donors instead of directly with the governments? Who is in charge of policy in these countries? Who is making the decisions? There may be good reasons for doing it this way, but it doesn't lead to trust and mutual influence. Governments generally tolerate this separate relationship, but most harbor suspicions about it. And it really puts the donors in a difficult, if not impossible situation. From the standpoint of the NGO, it's perfectly okay for donors to insist that a government adopt policies that an NGO is advocating. In fact, that's what the NGO is seeking when it approaches a donor. The same insistence becomes coercion and "violation of sovereignty" when the donor insists on a policy the NGO opposes. The only way out of this situation for donors is to encourage more NGO contact directly with government policymakers and make contacts between NGOs and donors a normal part of a three-way dialog that includes the government.

### Playing to the Home Audience

But this still only resolves part of the issues surrounding the involvement of special interest groups in the development agenda and their influence over donor agencies. Many international NGOs, along with commercial interests and even other government agencies, lobby legislators to change the criteria for aid decisions and use. In a number of countries, these efforts have succeeded in establishing fairly rigid guidelines or placing legal restrictions on the use of aid. As a consequence, donor agencies do not enjoy autonomy. Donor staff from countries where aid decisions have become politicized are at least as worried about the politics back home as they are about what's happening in the African country. The ambassador from a country where aid decisions are still relatively shielded from public debate told me: "My country does not openly complain to the government here; we privately complain. It's a quiet approach. Other donor countries are not allowed by their parliaments to be quiet." An ambassador from a Scandinavian country confirmed this: "My country has to play to the domestic audience back home and to public debate. You have to combine a critical stance on issues—sometimes in public—with a supportive role with the government here so that you can have influence. You have to balance between support for the government and for critics of the government. Balancing this is very difficult."

Nowhere has this been more evident than in the donors' stance on governance. Virtually all aid agencies are now paying increased attention to governance issues. As we discussed earlier, the agenda is very broad. It includes fighting corruption, improving government transparency and accountability, carrying out civil service reform, and encouraging multiparty democracy. Each donor country has its own ideas about what is the most important, what is the most urgent, and how it should be carried out. Increasingly, these ideas are formed by public debate and legislative fiat in the donor countries. Many of these ideas are formed without specific knowledge or even reference to specific country situations. Many assume—or, at least, act as if—African countries are already full-blown democracies.

Just as one swallow does not make a spring, neither does one election make a democracy. Leaving aside philosophical differences, which are not inconsiderable, African governments are faced with multiple and sometimes conflicting demands to improve governance, with varying degrees of practicality and realism. The differing mandates and views of the donor agencies are confusing, to say the least. Also, given complex internal political situations, an African government's degree of freedom to act is limited—even when there are no philosophical differences. Public debate and legislative oversight also increasingly circumscribe the freedom of donor agencies. A situation in which both parties have severe limitations is one where the dialog will be strained and difficult at best. No wonder governance matters are perceived by both African governments and donors as having brought new tensions into the relationship—tensions that are spilling over into less contentious aspects of the relationship. The increased role of legislatures and the accompanying politicization of aid decisions—meant to increase aid effectiveness—in practice is having the opposite effect. It is highly questionable whether the donors' involvement in political governance matters is having a positive effect, particularly in those circumstances where governments are managing complex political transitions. Meanwhile, the related tensions may well be constraining the donors' ability to positively influence other aspects of the development agenda.

### Agency Squabbles at Home

In addition to the limits placed on donor agencies by public opinion and legislatures, donor agency staff frequently must also contend with internal controversies. Rivalries and differing views between aid ministries and foreign ministries are common in a number of countries. In the United States, the State Department, the Treasury Department, and the Agency for International Development are all key actors in aid decisions. Depending on the issue, other agencies, such as the Environmental Protection Agency or the Commerce Department, are also involved. Unless and until a decision has been made on the U.S. government position—frequently a lengthy process—it is not uncommon for staff from the various agencies to make their views known—to each other, other donors, and the African government in question.

Confusion is one inevitable by-product. Another—loss of credibility for the official whose view ultimately does not prevail—is even potentially more damaging. Having witnessed ambassadors and other donor representatives espouse views that turn out not to be the official position of their governments, African government officials have become more than a little skeptical. One senior African official told me that, despite the extra work, his government welcomed visits from abroad by senior aid officials, in part because they were a good way of checking the reliability of what they had been hearing from the local representative. "If they mention it, I know it's an issue. If they tell me it's the position, then I know it's the position and not just the personal views of their man here." The frustration of African governments caught in these internal debates is mirrored in the frustration of the donor staff who operate in an atmosphere fraught with uncertainty.

### Foreign Policy versus Development

Over the last few years, there has been an increasing tendency for foreign ministries in donor countries to get more involved in development issues. In the United States, this resulted in the Agency for International Development (AID) being formally brought under the secretary of state, although AID still maintains a certain amount of autonomy. This tendency of foreign ministries to get more involved in aid matters has had several repercussions. Earlier on, we discussed how this has affected the *style* of the dialog. There are also repercussions for the *substance*. The first is confusion. Each donor country has its own configuration. Some have separate aid agencies that are either autonomous or report to a ministry of cooperation or development. Others have placed all aid decisions directly under the foreign ministry. Some have decentralized, placing authority for aid decisions with the ambassador, while others have not. New African governments spend precious time trying to figure out who's who and where the power lies with each donor.

The second more serious repercussion is the distortions that the increased role of foreign ministries brings to the development dialog. The first distortion affects the quality of the dialog. Few ambassadors or foreign ministry officials are economists, and few consider themselves to be development experts. Given this lack of training and experience, when charged with leading the dialog on economic and other issues, it is difficult for them to stray far from the "official line" and rigorously analyze the concerns and alternatives brought to the table by African governments. They may have staff who can help them, but frequently these staff are not there or not used. The African government officials understand that the ambassador is not really equipped to participate in a true dialog. The result is either a perfunctory exchange of views or the ambassador, in the interests of "good relations," takes at face value whatever the government is saying. Either way, a deep dialog on the issues is impossible and constructive mutual influence is out of the question.

The second distortion relates to the substance of the dialog. It is human nature for individuals to concentrate on those topics they know best. It is not surprising that political governance issues—such as the conduct of elections and relations with opposition political parties—have begun to dominate the development agenda and that economic matters and sector policies in more technical fields have been relegated, at least by some donors, to a back burner. Foreign ministries know politics; they don't know much about reducing poverty.

And the third distortion brought by the increasing role of foreign ministries in development matters is a shortened time frame. Ambassadors, like most politicians, tend to react to the here and now. The issue of the day becomes whatever is in the newspaper. As one ambassador remarked to me: "We get distracted by incidents; we don't look at the longer trends." When I complained to another ambassador about the lack of a long-term vision in a particular country, he said to me: "For me, a year *is* the long-term." So in Africa, most of the debate and dialog on aid, as well as the conditions set by donors, revolve around the next six to twelve months. Yet most development activities take years and need consistent support over the long haul. The short-term view of the ambassadors and other foreign ministry officials has begun to dominate the development dialog and comes into direct conflict with African perceptions of time touched upon in the last chapter.

### Donor Competition

In addition to internal rivalries and confusion *within* donors, there is also competition *among* donors. Political correctness in the development field dictates that donors now speak about partnerships and alliances for change. Donor coordination has become a central issue. Yet despite good intentions, rivalries and competition still exist. The amount of backbiting and gossip that takes place in diplomatic and development circles in African capitals is shocking. More seriously, there is intense jockeying for space to influence the government. Countries such as Mozambique that are considered to be good performers can only productively use a finite amount of money because of capacity constraints. In those countries, there is jockeying to ensure that the donor's entire aid allocation will be used. As one ambassador said to me: "The trouble is the cake is so small." Another donor representative said: "There is a conscious effort to improve coordination. . . . But I've seen really evil forms of competing here among donors. There is salary topping up and snatching up of each other's local staff. . . . When push comes to shove, they [the donors] put their own interests above cooperation. Each of them is competing for the government's attention." A donor representative had this to say about Nigeria when President Obasanjo returned to office: "Since the transition, the situation is like the wild west on donor coordination."

The competition and fear that one particular donor will become the "leading light" and get all the credit leads to perverse behavior. In one African country where HIV/AIDS is a raging epidemic, some donors were encouraging Ministry of Health officials to turn down a highly subsidized IDA credit from the World Bank for AIDS prevention and treatment. The rationale was that the IDA credit would contribute to the country's mounting debt and there would be sufficient grant funds available from other donors. The Minister of Finance had to step in and issue a press release reiterating the government's interest in the IDA credit. He reminded donors and some of his colleagues that the money needed to fight the AIDS epidemic in all likelihood far exceeded even the donors' collective capacity and his government was in need of urgent funds which had yet to materialize in substantial amounts from other donors.

What lay behind this incident was the feeling on the part of some donors that the World Bank was a Johnny-come-lately into the AIDS battle. By its sheer size and "enthusiasm," they feared it would wind up dominating the discussion, determining what the government's AIDS program would be, and stealing all the credit, even though other donors had been involved much earlier and would be expected to contribute funds. Whether or not the donors' suspicions are well founded is not the point. In either case, the blatant competition among donors and the ensuing confusion diverted time and attention away from the urgent matter at hand—fighting HIV/AIDS.

This anecdote should not be interpreted to mean that multilateral institutions, like the World Bank, are above the fray. Not at all. Like the others, they are part of the competition and rivalry that continue to hurt aid effectiveness. Some African governments attempt to use this to their advantage and play donors off against each another. These attempts generally bring only more confusion and less effectiveness. Where strong governments exist, they are able to provide leadership and contain competition, but they can't completely eliminate it. Also, since most African governments are not particularly strong in aid coordination, despite their best intentions and those of some aid officials, the competition continues.

### The Costs of Transparency

A final "big picture" factor affecting development effectiveness results from the increased transparency and opening up of aid agencies that began in the 1990s. The scrutiny from the media and NGO community has unquestionably been a positive factor. It has made aid agencies more responsive, less secretive, and more sensitive. Most of the issues discussed in this book would have been dismissed as irrelevant or unimportant without the greater public scrutiny brought about by NGOs and the press. Nonetheless, it is a double-edged sword, and there are also costs. Too often, NGOs launch campaigns or the press runs with stories that are full of incomplete or erroneous information. What makes a good story or what makes a good cause is not necessarily what development is all about. Development agency staff get frustrated when they see their hard work discounted or criticized without a full airing of the facts.

That is perhaps inevitable, and there is no reason for donor agencies to be exempt from public scrutiny and public criticism. But there may need to be limits. Individual development agency staff have been targeted in the press, in orchestrated NGO campaigns, and during university lectures and debates. Most development specialists do not seek the limelight. As one of them said to me: "If I wanted to be personally embroiled in controversy with my face in the newspaper, I would have become a politician."

Too bad or so what, you might say. But the real problem here is "once bitten, twice shy." Some excellent professionals have retired altogether from field operations rather than face relentless professional—and personal—criticism from the press or NGOs. Others have become overly cautious and excessively risk-adverse. That's the real danger. In order to avoid controversies, many donor staff now avoid the tough issues—and that's not only in public, but in private as well. And it's hard to blame them. It is not uncommon for the contents of official letters or meetings to be leaked to the press.

Maybe all of this does act as a safeguard against donors coercing governments into action, but it also gets in the way of trust and dialog and debate. And the NGO community and even the media don't seem to mind donor coercion if it supports the cause they're supporting, so it's unclear if this is really much of a deterrent to coercion. What is clear is that public attacks on development agencies and their staff create risk aversion, interfere with dialog and trust, and lessen the possibilities for mutual influence between African governments and donors. The transparent, Internet age comes at a price.

## INDIVIDUAL PRESSURES AND INCENTIVES AND THE WORK ENVIRONMENT

The beginning of this chapter dealt with the external and "big picture" factors that increasingly play a role in aid and the way that donors work. There are numerous sweeping trends—fluctuations in aid budgets, the quest for immediate results, restrictions on the use of aid, and the general politicization of aid with greater involvement by legislatures, special interests groups, and the media. Donor staff are not only caught up in this maelstrom, but must also contend with their own internal bureaucracies. In recent years, some of the aid agencies, particularly the international agencies such as the World Bank, IMF, and European Union, have been criticized for their plush working environments. Leaving aside the question of how "plush" the environments really are, it is important to look at internal work factors and incentives and how these affect the relationships between donors and African governments, and ultimately aid effectiveness.

The first thing that needs to be said is that not all development bureaucracies are alike. There are big differences. Some are decentralized; others have few staff in the field. Some are big; others are quite small. Some are prestigious places to work; others are dumping grounds for civil servants. Some have made considerable efforts to reform in recent years; others seem frozen in time. Much of what follows is not unique to international aid agencies or even the public sector. Some material is only relevant to the large, multinational aid bureaucracies. Nonetheless, most international aid specialists will be able to recognize and identify with much of what follows.

## Life in a Bureaucracy

The internal life of these bureaucracies is not all bad. Most employ highly qualified, motivated staff who are dedicated to helping the poor. In most agencies, there is a large degree of collegiality and esprit de corps. The work is professionally challenging, personally stimulating, and engrossing. It is no coincidence, for example, that staff entering the World Bank are said to be "joining" the Bank, and that the trips they go on are described as "missions." Few people fall into this line of work; most have made a conscious choice and a commitment. A former staff member of the World Bank described it as a "total institution." Most staff who have stayed a number of years can trace many of their personal and professional connections back to the institution.

Yet in most development agencies today, there is also an air of disenchantment and cynicism. Staff morale is not uniformly high. The reasons for this include external pressures on the work environment, internal bureaucratic behaviors and norms, and individual psychological pressures. While many of these are not unique to donors and development agencies, the combination serves to distract attention from the work directly with the countries.

The external pressures on staff working in development agencies are a result of the trends discussed earlier in this chapter. Skepticism about aid effectiveness, fluctuating aid budgets, growing demands and mandates, coupled with globalization's push for leaner, more efficient businesses, have resulted in staff having to "do more with less." Accompanying this is a loss of benefits, "perks," and status in some agencies. It seems almost ridiculous to complain about any of this—particularly for those charged with working for the world's destitute and getting paid pretty well for doing so. But these pressures combine to evoke feelings of worthlessness and lack of appreciation in staff. The nature of development work is such that it is difficult to see immediate results and failure is far from unknown. When you couple this with constant criticism in the press and from NGOs, it is hard to maintain a sense of self-esteem and professional pride. Loss of benefits, perks, or status, consciously or unconsciously, only reinforces this.

Why does this matter? It matters because, as many MBA students learn, employee satisfaction is one of the best proxies for customer satisfaction. It matters because feelings of personal worth and competence, what Peter Senge calls personal mastery, are linked to organizational effectiveness. In his words, "Organizations learn only through individuals who learn. Individual learning does not guarantee organizational learning. But without it, no organizational learning occurs."[9] If donor agencies and African governments are to listen and learn from each other, it's critical that donor staff feel a sense of personal mastery and personal worth. A supportive internal environment in the development agencies could help to counterbalance the negative effects of the external pressures and their consequences. That doesn't mean providing big offices for everyone, huge bonuses, or restoring perks, but rather reinforcing the message that staff efforts are appreciated. And that goes for all staff and not just the select few who receive awards and recognition. It also means creating a work environment that is perceived to be fair, and one that provides staff with the necessary tools and incentives to establish a better relationship with African governments.

### Battling the Bureaucracy

The work environment in at least some donor agencies today hardly fits that description. Bureaucratic barriers were cited over and over by development officials as an important obstacle to doing a better job or having a better relationship with African governments. While officials from some European countries felt that there had been significant improvements in their agencies over the last few years, most aid officials complained of endless bureaucracy and complex procedures. As one aid official put it: "We sink in our own rules and procedures. The speed and quality of our response is not good enough." Another said: "There is bureaucratic, centralized decision-making in my agency . . . and the internal discussion gets tied up in minutiae. . . . We are slow, faddish, and depend on the whim of a minister."

Efforts to streamline bureaucracy are being made in nearly all the aid institutions. But in agencies like the World Bank and European Union, project preparation and approval can still take years. The internal demands are such that they take on a life of their own. Anxieties over aid effectiveness have made this problem worse as agencies struggle to implement complex monitoring systems in order to "prove" their efficiency or the quality of their work. As one World Bank country director said to me: "We seem to be managing by the numbers. We are living by indicators." But are those indicators measuring the right things? With the exception of a few questions that are part of client surveys carried out every couple of years by some agencies, few, if any, of the indicators are concerned with the quality of dialog and the relationship between donor staff and their African colleagues. As Peter Senge noted: "Because service quality is intangible, there is a strong tendency to manage service businesses by focusing on what is most tangible. But focusing on what's easily measured leads to 'looking good without being good.'"[10] It also leads to the classic bureaucratic behavior of avoiding risks that "won't look good in the numbers." The common complaint voiced by staff in many development agencies rings true: feeding the beast is getting in the way of serving the client.

This tendency is being exacerbated by the latest push to implement results-based aid. A number of donors, including the United States, have conditioned additional aid, whether bilateral aid or increased contributions to multilateral aid agencies, on aid agencies' ability to show concrete progress against agreed goals and targets. In 2000, as part of the millennium celebrations and deliberations, members of the United Nations, along with multilateral development agencies like the World Bank, agreed on a set of Millennium Development Goals (MDGs). Results-based aid and the MDGs are a step in the right direction. Instead of focusing on a specific set of inputs, activities, and projects over the short-term, the MDGs focus on achieving concrete results over the medium term, for example, universal primary education for boys and girls alike by 2015. They counteract past tendencies to measure progress in terms of inputs, for example, dollars spent or teachers trained, instead of focusing on achievements and outcomes, like educational levels. But, the clear danger is that constant pressures on aid budgets and agencies' anxiety to show their effectiveness and role in achieving the MDGs will generate a whole new "counting and measurement industry" and a push to "show the numbers." Although the MDGs are meant to hale a new partnership for development among donors and aid recipients—and are a start toward measuring the right things—given short-term political realities in the donor countries, and limited time and resources in aid agencies, dialog and aid relationships could well be casualties.

In addition to complicated procedures and weighty internal requirements, many of the aid agencies, particularly the larger ones, have a culture that is inwardly focused and not conducive to building relationships and trust. Many of the staff are highly educated. Most of their experience reinforces an appreciation of individual excellence and success. Teamwork and team success—with dialog, mutual cooperation, and trust as essential ingredients—are held in lower esteem. For a large portion of the staff, teamwork is associated with delays, long debates, and mediocre results as the interests and views of every-one are somehow accommodated.

When it's clear what to do and how to do it, and an individual has the req-uisite skills, it may well be faster and better for one person to tackle the task. But in development work it is seldom clear exactly what to do or how to do it, and it is nearly impossible for one individual to have all the requisite skills and knowledge. So it's fairly evident in those circumstances that teamwork pos-sesses a distinct advantage. Unless and until development agencies are able to foster teamwork internally, it is unlikely that they will be able to foster team-work externally, most importantly with African governments, but also with other donors. And until then, some of the most valued staff—those who are highly qualified and experienced—will be less effective than they can be and labeled as impatient and arrogant.

The inward-looking nature of most aid bureaucracies manifests itself in other ways. Reputations can be made and broken in meetings. There is a high premium placed on the ability to speak well internally and play to one's peers. This verbal football places women and other minorities at a distinct disad-vantage. More importantly, it is not a good predictor as to whether a staff member can communicate successfully with African officials and others who don't necessarily share the same educational level or intellectual paradigm. Similarly, writing good reports is highly valued. Until the last few years, there was little attention paid as to who would read the reports outside of one's peers. A number of development agencies still have reports that are not acces-sible to African governments and the public, either because they are consid-ered to be confidential or because they are written in a language not commonly understood in the African country. While there has been great progress in increasing public access to reports and other information, not enough has been done to make these user-friendly. Many donor staff would join in my confession that after reading literally thousands of reports over the course of a long career, I *still* find them difficult to read.

Perhaps most telling about the inward-nature of the aid industry is the sur-prise that many aid agency staff felt at being targets of antiglobalization protests. Many staff at the World Bank were genuinely shaken by the vehe-mence of the antiglobalization demonstrations during the spring 2000 meet-ings held in Washington, D.C. Before that, globalization and its implications were hardly mentioned internally, at least at the working levels. And while staff knew that certain groups were unhappy with specific policies and projects that the World Bank supported, it seemed to many that a worldwide movement had sprung up around them almost overnight without their noticing. And it made staff realize how little the public actually knew about what happens in the "development world," including the World Bank. At the same time, more than one staff commented that the things being said on the outside were similar to what we were saying on the inside. The antiglobalization movement served as both a mirror and a window to aid agency staff.

### Personnel Policies

Some agencies are trying to open up internal perspectives by hiring a more diverse set of officials. For country agencies, this generally means hiring more women and more local staff in the field. International agencies, in addition to those groups, are also looking for more people who come from third world countries. Progress has been made in this area over the last several years, but most aid agencies remain dominated by the "white male syndrome"—even those, I hasten to add, that are led by women at the top. Even where women and minorities are present in increasing numbers, there persists a "macho" culture. All the old clichés—"playing hardball . . . never let them see you sweat . . . you have to show them you mean business"—are still in full bloom. Successful women and minorities generally imitate this behavior and sooner or later, get sucked into it. It is not a culture that prides itself on dialog and seeing both sides of an issue. It is a culture that seems to thrive on confrontation and hard-driving negotiation. It is a culture that needs to change if dialog and trust—and hence, mutual influence—are going to be established with African governments.

*Management Quality*   While hiring policies are going in the right direction, albeit slowly, it's difficult to say that about many other personnel policies. Staff in development agencies constantly complain about the quality of leadership and management. Although there are many talented managers and leaders, it's not hard to understand why there are complaints. In some donor agencies, promotions are based largely on political considerations, so it's not uncommon to find managers who do not have the qualifications. More often than not, however, it's the opposite problem. Staff are promoted into management positions based on their qualifications and past experience, which may have been largely technical. Being a superb macroeconomist or urban planner does not necessarily make you an inspiring leader or adept at having a dialog with high-level African officials. Training can help, but as most managers will tell you, it generally comes too little, too late. Most managers in development agencies are put into place with little or no relevant training, even in conventional management skills, let alone in the more complex leadership qualities needed to improve aid effectiveness. Some agencies, including the World Bank, are now trying to change this, but it is too soon to tell if the new leadership programs are effective.

*Stigma of Africa*   A final problem with the selection of managers in development agencies involves the professional taint that working on Africa has acquired because of its weak economic performance and the poor results of aid. This does not hold true for some bilateral donor agencies where Africa is the focus of development efforts. But for many of the agencies, working on Africa is not viewed as the most prestigious appointment. So whom does it attract? It attracts young first-time managers, some of whom are highly talented and are quickly whisked away to other assignments. Others use Africa as their training ground. Africa also attracts about-to-retire and middle-of-the-road managers who are unlikely to take big risks or break out of "old-style" relationships. In some cases, Africa is also the destination for those who made mistakes in more illustrious assignments. It's a dead giveaway when an ambassador who has first served as an ambassador in a non-African country comes to serve as an ambassador to an African country. But it needs to be underscored that Africa also attracts the truly committed: there are managers and leaders in development agencies who continue to work on Africa tirelessly and with the hope that some of the breakthroughs discussed in this book—establishing relationships of trust and mutual influence and consequently, achieving effective poverty reduction—can happen.

*Staff*   How about the staff who work on Africa? Not surprisingly, the staff are a mirror image of the managers. There are the young and talented stars who make a brief appearance. There are the new hires. There are the "old African hands" who know a lot, but who are not about to make waves. And there are also the truly dedicated and competent ones.

Quite aside from some quality issues, which are worse in smaller countries and those requiring foreign language skills, there is a relatively high turnover of staff who work on Africa. The young ones, once trained, go elsewhere. The older ones retire. Staff continuity, an absolute must for dialog and relationship building, is poor. Other organizational policies have tended to exacerbate this problem of staff continuity. Several agencies, including the World Bank, have matrix organizations with country desks and pools of technical specialists. The technical specialists have no "country home," but are contracted as needed by the country desks. This type of organization was meant to reinforce technical excellence, as technical specialists could easily work across boundaries and bring experience from one country to another. The trouble is that it may be working too well. Large countries can afford to "buy" full-time technical specialists, but smaller countries share technical specialists with as many as four or five other countries. Under those circumstances, when a technical specialist visits a country infrequently only for a few days at a time, it is virtually impossible to establish the kind of relationship that leads to mutual influence. The specialist doesn't really understand the country conditions, and the country's officials seldom absorb the technical advice being proffered. And those assignments are subject to frequent change.

A number of agencies have also offered enhanced early retirement benefits or severance pay and benefit packages to volunteers in efforts to trim staff and/or bring in new blood. The problem with those programs is that there is often a self-selection that rids the agency of some of its most experienced staff, sometimes at the point of peak performance. These voluntary retirement programs may not be a bad idea. But they contribute to increasing the overall rate of staff turnover and hence, to the African governments' impression that they seldom see the same face more than once or twice. Also contributing are the tight budgets. Because there is little slack in the system, one staff departure frequently sets off a chain reaction of multiple staff movements.

I realize that the personnel picture I have painted is fairly bleak. Successful and experienced managers and staff from elsewhere in the organization look at Africa as a "backwater" where there is a likelihood of getting stuck working on "hopeless" countries. They want to be associated with success, so they avoid working on Africa. Some agencies are aware of the problem and are looking at promotion criteria and other possible incentives, but, so far, there are no serious programs in place. So while there are dedicated and competent staff, it isn't clear that the development agencies have enough of the kind of staff needed to sustain a process of dialog and maintain relationships based on trust and mutual influence.

## Vertical and Horizontal Structures

Another issue in the work environment within donor agencies revolves around "vertical" and "horizontal" communication and coordination. Vertical communication occurs between staff residing in an African country and those located at headquarters. Horizontal communication occurs between different parts of the organization. Not surprisingly, vertical coordination has proven to be quite difficult. Staff in the field complain that managers and other specialists from headquarters don't know the country context. Staff at headquarters complain that their field colleagues have lost their objectivity; they have "gotten too close" to the problems. As a consequence of different perspectives, it is not uncommon for headquarters and field staff to have different positions or recommendations on issues. This affects agency capacity to dialog with African governments in two separate ways. First and most obviously, it confuses government officials and injects a permanent air of uncertainty in the relationship. At least some of the problems associated with unreliability can be traced back to vertical issues. Less obviously, problems in vertical communication and coordination result in infighting that robs time from the dialog and contributes to lower staff morale. While agencies have tried to resolve vertical issues by delegating clear authority and decision-making responsibilities to the field, in many instances the problems persist.

Similar problems occur with horizontal communication and coordination, particularly in the larger agencies. It is not uncommon for staff and consultants working on one project in a country to know very little about related work on another project also being supported by their agency. Staff who work on specific technical matters generally know little about macroeconomic issues, even though the latter can have major effects on a project's chances for success. And it goes the other way too. Many economists know little about issues such as those related to education and health that can have major effects on a nation's overall economic development, as the HIV/AIDS epidemic has sadly demonstrated.

No one can really be a jack of all trades, and it is unrealistic to expect this. But many issues facing developing countries today are multifaceted, requiring integrated technical advice adapted to specific country circumstances. A number of agencies have reorganized themselves or created teams in an effort to increase the information flow and teamwork among staff working on the same country. The 1997 reorganization of the World Bank included the appointment of country directors with the explicit responsibility to create and foster country teams and ensure that activities within each country were fully integrated and known to all. This effort has clearly helped, but the 1997 reorganization also created a matrix organization with large pools of technical staff. As noted earlier, few staff are able to dedicate all of their efforts to only one or two countries. So most technical staff have little time and see relatively little payoff in making the kind of investment needed to become active country team members and learn what is happening in the country. Problems of horizontal communication and coordination persist and add to both donor and African government frustrations.

### Personal Issues

To close this chapter on institutional constraints, let's come back for a moment to the individuals who work for donor agencies on Africa. In addition to the external pressures and internal bureaucratic problems that make the job increasingly difficult, there are also issues of an individual or personal nature. The job unquestionably involves sacrifices. For most officials, there are frequent and/or long stays away from their families. Life is filled with a need for breathtaking organization and logistics. For example, the dilemma of attending a ministerial meeting in Africa and being at home for a daughter's birthday or a spouse's surgery is not just a one-time occurrence. For those working in development, this type of balancing and juggling is a career-long problem. Some staff try to resolve these issues by taking in-country assignments, and sometimes this helps. But those assignments involve different kinds of tradeoffs, including exposing families to greater health and security risks, and affording children fewer formal educational opportunities. All people who work engage in balancing acts, but the nature of development work usually means that the tradeoffs are more serious and more frequent.[11]

In addition to work/family pressures, staff feel other psychological pressures. Some donor staff are extroverted and have excellent people skills. Many others, however, were employed on the basis of their technical skills and analytical abilities. It is a real struggle for those staff to exercise the interpersonal skills needed to really engage their African colleagues. They may try, and some succeed, but it takes a tremendous personal toll. Also taking a tremendous personal toll is being caught in the position of being the "development specialist" who supposedly has the answers to alleviate human suffering. It is easy for staff to become depressed or feel powerless when confronted with the failure of most development efforts in Africa, coupled with the scarcity of "short-term wins" or easy fixes to African problems. Work-related stress is an ongoing challenge.

So the glamorous image of the jet-setting development specialist constantly off on glorious adventures is not exactly an accurate picture. Why does this matter? It matters because the profession, particularly in Africa, must be able to attract and maintain professionals who not only arrive committed, but who can *stay* committed. After years of being buffeted by external pressures, surviving the internal bureaucracy, and managing complex work/personal tradeoffs, it is perhaps surprising how many staff continue to keep up their dedication and morale. But it is increasingly unrealistic to expect staff caught up in all these pressures to take the time and make the efforts needed to really engage African government officials in dialog and a process of mutual influence. And that tells us that development institutions need to change how they deal with both external pressures and internal organizational matters if aid effectiveness is to increase. We will look at some possible changes in the next chapter.

## NOTES

1. The G-7 meets periodically and takes a common stand on a wide range of economic and political issues. The members of the G-7 are the United States, Canada, Great Britain, France, Germany, Japan, and Italy. In the post-Soviet era, Russia has been invited to G-7 meetings, and in those instances, the group has become known as the G-8.

2. World Bank Staff Survey 2003 conducted in the last quarter of 2003. The overall survey response rate was also high, at 83 percent.

3. World Bank Staff Survey. A similar survey conducted in 2002 reported even higher impact on staff, with 44 percent reporting that work pressures had affected their health over the preceding year.

4. Even in agencies such as the World Bank that do not have fixed lending or commitment allocations for each country each year, the same dynamic plays itself out through the administrative budget allocated to the country desk.

5. See also Easterly 2002, especially the section on "Redefining output."

6. As Carol Lancaster points out, this is not homogenous. Some countries and their legislatures are more aid friendly or exercise less direct influence; others, like the United States, are reluctant aid-givers and congressional debates directly influence the size and conditions for aid. See Lancaster 1999, especially chapter 5 on the United States.

7. Easterly 2002 also discusses the need for "observable outputs."

8. Integrated rural development projects are *horizontally integrated* area-based projects, usually financed by one donor, that can have up to twenty different activities (e.g., health, education, agricultural extension, rural roads) within the same project. Sector investment programs are *vertically integrated* programs encompassing all government-supported activities and all major donors within a given sector such as agriculture or education.

9. Senge 1994, p. 139.

10. Senge 1994, p. 333.

11. Stress and work/life balance were signaled as problem areas in both the 2002 and 2003 World Bank staff surveys. For example, some 44 percent of staff in 2003 felt they did not have sufficient flexibility to meet personal or family needs.

# Tearing Down the Wall: Can Aid Relationships Be Improved?

The events of September 11, 2001, starkly underlined the interdependent relationship between the rich and the poor, the haves and the have-nots. People all over the world discovered, in a matter of moments, that events in far away, isolated countries like Afghanistan can have a dramatic impact on daily life. This may not have been news to the poor countries in Africa. They have understood for years that much of their welfare depends on events and decisions taken in the major capitals of the world. But it did come as a bit of a shock to many, especially in the United States. James Wolfensohn, the World Bank president, has noted that for too long an imaginary wall separated the rich world from the poor. He went on to say: "There is no wall. We are linked by trade, investment, finance, by travel and communications, by disease, by crime, by migration, by environmental degradation, by drugs, by financial crises and by terror."[1] And, of course, by aid. The question facing African governments, and especially the international aid community, is whether business will continue as usual. If it does, Africa at best is likely to become increasingly irrelevant in the global system, or at worst, the cradle of the world's conflicts and epidemics.

Instead of examining the substance of aid-financed programs and the specific conditions surrounding aid today, this book has focused on the relationship between donors and African governments. The argument is simple. If aid effectiveness is to improve, then the relationship needs to be transformed from one of suspicion and coercion to one of *mutual influence and trust.* The psychological wall separating donors and aid recipients needs to be removed. Under today's rules of the game, African governments have temporarily complied with donor rules and conditions for a few months or years. Individual projects or programs have succeeded, but despite billions of dollars of aid—and successes elsewhere—sustained economic growth and poverty reduction have eluded the majority of these countries.

That's a powerful argument for change and even radical change, both of which are easy to say, but extremely difficult to do. Good relationships and trust cannot be mandated or wished into existence; they must grow. And unfortunately, it's not as simple as just having donors drive aid ("if they would only listen to us—we know what works") or giving governments carte blanche and a blank check ("just give us the money—we know what to do"). There are plenty of examples of both in the past, with scant evidence of success. And as we have seen in the preceding pages, the environment for nurturing trust is not optimal. Questions abound about the extent of shared values and commitment between African governments and donors, along with a perceived lack of reliability that is closely tied to institutional problems. Deep-rooted cultural differences and communication problems also contribute.

Most aid critiques focus mainly, if not exclusively, on the sins of recipient governments. This critique argues that the problems are a two-way street, and that problems on the donor side are also substantial. In light of long experience, it is tempting to throw up one's hands in despair and declare the situation hopeless. In fact that's what most aid critics do—they trash the industry and move on.

Is the situation hopeless? Not entirely. There are a number of ideas floating around in the aid industry that could improve the situation, and we will look at some in this chapter. We should recognize from the outset, however, that there is little hope that these ideas will be adopted and fully implemented unless donors are prepared to make some profound shifts in the way they do business. Piecemeal changes will work exactly as their name implies.

So, let's go back to the supporting and core elements of trust we discussed earlier and talk about ongoing efforts and new proposals that could strengthen each of these elements. Finally, we will draw some conclusions as to the "state of the industry" and the prospects for improved aid effectiveness through improved aid relationships.

## SUPPORTING ELEMENTS OF TRUST: FAMILIARITY, TRANSPARENCY, AND OPEN AND HONEST COMMUNICATION

The supporting elements of trust—familiarity, transparency, and open and honest communication—are more process-oriented, and in a sense, easier to fix than the core elements of shared purpose, commitment, and reliability. Even without radical changes in the aid industry, these are elements that are amenable to gradual improvements. Indeed, substantial changes have taken place in the last decade. Brought on by frank self-appraisals and criticism by the antiglobalization movement—and by the collective introspection following the World Trade Center attack—the aid industry is undergoing a period of questioning and some change. Whether change will be fast enough or radical enough to make a real difference in aid effectiveness is the central issue.

### Familiarity

More rapid and easy communication, mass media such as CNN, and the changes in South Africa have "opened up" Africa to millions of people in donor countries. Yet nine times out of ten, the stories in the Western media are negative. What are the African stories getting media attention as the new century unfolds? AIDS, child soldiers in Sierra Leone, continuing trouble in the Congo, famine in southern Africa, and violence and electoral shenanigans in Zimbabwe and elsewhere. Are there positive stories being reported internationally? Only two spring to mind—peaceful second elections in South Africa and the international debt relief program. And both of these frequently have negative or critical undertones. What the public understands about Africa is that it's a continent of turmoil, disease, desperate poverty, and hopelessness.

*Media Objectivity* Western media need to begin balancing their coverage of Africa—reporting today on Africa is nothing short of irresponsible. Other countries besides South Africa are slowly beginning the process of building a democracy. Stories of hope have emerged all over the continent—children attending school, AIDS prevention programs, rich cultural traditions, unique and breathtaking art and music, community wildlife preservation programs, valuable natural resources, and radical economic transformations. It is not true, as some media claim, that the positive stories are boring or "not newsworthy." In each positive or hopeful story, there is enough drama to satisfy even the most avid thrill seeker. We cannot expect more of the politicians who have power over aid agencies and development assistance to Africa unless more is done to educate the general public. And the responsibility for this rests squarely with the media.

*Staff Education*    Along with more public education, donor agencies themselves must invest in staff education. Among the donors, most provide little or no specific training on the African countries to which their staff are assigned. There are some exceptions—among others, Denmark and Sweden have country training programs that include cultural aspects; the United States runs courses for diplomats at its Foreign Service Institute; Great Britain's Foreign Office makes some training available, mainly to diplomats; and the United Nations runs familiarization programs in some countries for its staff. The vast majority of aid personnel, whether staff or consultants, arrive in an African country with little or no specific knowledge of the country's history and cultural traditions, or even recent political and economic events. It is an irony of the aid business that high-level donor officials who visit an African country for a day or two usually receive extensive oral and written briefings, while the staff assigned to work on the country mainly rely on informal contacts with other staff and whatever reports come their way. And this applies both to staff sent to live in the country, as well as traveling staff and consultants.

This needs to change. One solution is to have each donor develop its own in-house, country-specific (or subregional) training program. This type of training can also serve to strengthen information exchanges and teamwork among the staff and consultants working in a country. A second solution is to develop a multidonor, country-specific training program for all donor staff working on a particular country. Different donors could take responsibility for different countries, or they could agree to ask a multilateral institution such as the European Commission, United Nations, or World Bank Institute to develop and carry out this multidonor training on a regular basis. This would have the added benefit of contributing to better donor coordination. But by far the simplest and best solution would be for each African government, with donor funds and assistance as necessary, to develop and present a training course on history, cultural traditions, and recent political and economic events for all donor staff working in the country. International investors and NGO staff could also be included. Once developed, the course could be repeated quarterly or semiannually for the newcomers.

*Government-Donor Courses*    A related idea is for governments and donors to develop joint courses, where government and donor staff sit together and receive the same training. This type of training could cover a lot of ground—discussing cultural differences and historical events, acquiring jointly needed skills such as negotiation techniques, and analyzing concrete issues and problems in the country's current development program. Not only would donor and government staff begin to know one another and understand the legitimacy of differing perceptions and perspectives, but they could acquire a common set of tools and language. Psychologically, they would be placed on a common footing, as classmates rather than teachers and pupils.

Do these recommendations cost money? Yes. But any of the multidonor training schemes, especially ones developed and carried out in the country, would be relatively inexpensive. The biggest expense would be the staff time spent attending the course instead of attending to "business." If you consider the consistent feedback from African governments that donors simply don't understand their people or their country's specific history or conditions, it seems clear that "business" will benefit.

*Decentralization*   What about decentralization and moving more staff to the field? As we discussed in chapter 2, decentralization is a double-edged sword. Staff living in a country have a much greater opportunity to become familiar with the country and interact on a regular basis with citizens from all walks of life. It also helps with the problem of staff continuity since resident staff generally stay for two or three years. But the other side of the coin is the risk of micromanagement and interference in the daily workings of government; the presence of mediocre or unmotivated staff; and the distortions of expatriates living in a "glass bubble" (you can see and hear faintly, but there is little real interaction). And decentralization, without constant efforts to shore up internal coordination within agencies, could further undermine perceptions of donor reliability and the overall relationship.

Improved selection and training, as well as consciousness and clarity about resident staff roles, can help the situation. Hiring national staff and having a blend of local and international staff can also help. The World Bank and the United Nations Development Program, for example, are increasingly using this model. But given the present state of the aid relationship, moving large numbers of staff to Africa must be approached with caution. In too many cases, it is other donors rather than the government that are anxious to have more donor staff in the field. One motivation is to have adequate staffing to attend the endless donor coordination meetings that take place—many without the presence of the government. Another is to ensure that donor-funded programs are being properly implemented. But having too many resident staff clearly leaves the impression that development belongs to the donor, and is not the domain of the government and its citizens. Ironically, as many donors have increased the size of their in-country offices, others (sometimes even the same donor) are using fewer long-term resident foreign advisers, based on earlier critiques and the limited capacity-building that actually took place.

When governments talk about decentralization of donor agencies, they mean something different. Most government officials argue for authority and decision making to be decentralized to local donor representatives. Sometimes this is based on a perception that frequent interaction can lead to greater influence on their donor colleagues, and bringing the locus of decision making closer brings them one step closer to managing their own affairs. But mostly it seems to be an affirmation of government views that aid agencies are calling the shots and that their internal decision-making processes are generally slow and opaque. Decentralization at least allows them to put a face and name to the problem.

Ideally, decentralization of authority and decision making can foster better relationships through increased dialog and building trust, but there needs to be clarity about roles and the aid relationship. Remember the government officials in chapter 3 who said that some diplomats overstepped their roles. And remember that in present circumstances, many ambassadors and country representatives of aid agencies get caught up in short-term pressures—some generated far from the country—and become too focused on short-term results. Unless other fundamental aspects of the aid business and the relationship change, decentralization alone will not improve the situation. Some efforts, for example, moving massive numbers of staff to the field, could make the situation worse. Decentralization is no panacea for what ails the aid industry.

### Transparency

Transparency is an area where there has been considerable progress over the past few years. Increased transparency has largely resulted from external pressure from NGOs and legislatures. The value of transparency and open communication, however, has not always been internalized by donors and their staff. Consequently, contradictions abound. For example, some bilateral aid donors are vocal advocates of increased transparency, more public consultation, and greater openness on the part of the World Bank and IMF. Some of these same donors don't necessarily practice what they preach. Many bilateral annual consultations with governments still take place in today's equivalent of smoke-filled rooms with little systematic participation or consultation with other interested parties. And bilateral strategies, policy documents, and mission reports are not nearly as public or readily available as those from the World Bank.

So while the World Bank, European Commission, and the IMF must keep moving forward on transparency, there is also a need for bilateral agencies to catch up. More bilateral aid documents need to be readily accessible to African government officials and the public, and annual consultation processes between bilateral donors and governments need to be reformed and opened up to public consultation and scrutiny. The way it works today, a delegation of senior aid officials descends on an African country for a few days and holds high-level, closed-door discussions. Some make the effort to meet some NGOs or private-sector representatives, but nongovernment representatives are seldom, if ever, an integral part of the decision-making discussions. The impression, if not the reality, is an aura of secrecy, punctuated only by some headlines in the local newspaper about how much money the donor will be giving to the country in the following year.

Transparency should also be a central concern when aid decisions are decentralized to ambassadors and local heads of aid agencies. While this type of decentralization can streamline and speed up aid decisions, those decisions should not be exempt from public discussion and scrutiny. If they are, there is the real danger that aid programs will be a shopping list drawn up during private conversations between a minister or two and the donor representative. While sometimes this can result in just-in-time assistance, more often than not the programs and projects do not focus on priority issues or run into difficulties because they lack more general support, even from other members of the government.

Transparency by the donors is important and can also generate increased transparency and openness on the part of African governments. Public donor strategy documents, based on government policies, can create a climate where governments are willing to share more of their internal thinking not only with donors, but also with the public at large. There are new efforts underway that can provide opportunities for the programs of both African governments and donors to become more transparent. One of these is the Poverty Reduction Strategy Paper (PRSP). The PRSP is a government document prepared by each country in consultation with donors and the public, which maps out the country's poverty program. The PRSP is now a prerequisite for IMF and World Bank program lending and donor debt relief. PRSPs potentially can also be an important tool to clarify and agree on objectives, a subject to which we will return later.

Meanwhile, transparency begins at home. Donor staff need to know the status of important pending decisions and how their agency works—when and where decisions get made and by whom. Staff need to understand that part of their jobs is not only dealing with the subjects of their expertise, but also being able to accurately describe the process of decision making to their government colleagues. This is particularly important for donor staff who reside in the countries. Too often, they feel—and convey—that their agencies back home are "black boxes" where information goes in but nothing much comes out. Part of this is perception, part is real. Aid agencies need to invest more in adequately briefing their staff and managers—again, a fairly low-cost proposition with potentially high returns. At the same time, a number of aid agencies *are* black boxes. Unless procedures and practices can be simplified, it becomes an almost impossible task for staff to understand and accurately convey how decisions are made and why.

Doing something to further transparency as discussed above is certainly within the grasp of aid agencies. It is, in fact, not much of a reach, and many are already heading in that direction. For example, in mid-2001, the World Bank appointed a director for internal communications. Staff, for the first time, now have access to timely information about what is happening internally within the organization, and about the efforts of the World Bank to link up with broader international initiatives. Thanks to modern technology, all staff have to do is click once on their desktop computers. But there are other important recommendations surrounding transparency that are more difficult to implement.

*Aid Transparency*    The first is to make nondevelopment aid decisions more transparent. Long after the Cold War, many aid decisions are still prompted by other concerns, with security concerns and commercial interests leading the way. And today, with the newly declared war on international terrorism, this trend is likely to increase. At the very least, the basis for aid decisions should be more transparent. It is impossible to expect development impact and concrete poverty reduction from aid targeted at a central objective that is clearly something else. For a combination of reasons, this type of aid often masquerades as development aid, a charade that hurts transparency and consequently undermines trust, since those closest to the situation are not fooled.

Nowhere is this more evident than in the use of tied aid, where aid is offered only in the form of goods and services from the donor country. As recently as 2001, over 70 percent of United States foreign aid was tied, and a number of European countries, including Italy, Germany, Denmark, Sweden, and France, still tied one-third or more of their aid.[2] Too often, the donor benefits more from tied aid than does the recipient. Either way, tied aid leaves the impression of a murky business, where motives are different from stated objectives and where transparency and open competition are sacrificed. Despite recommendations from respected multilateral institutions such as the Organization for Economic Cooperation and Development (OECD) and the lead of some European countries such as Great Britain—which announced that it was terminating the use of tied aid in December 2000—movement on this issue has been uneven at best. The OECD recommendation on untying aid to the least developed countries was reiterated and formally agreed to by OECD members in May 2001. The call to untie aid was renewed at the March 2002 International Conference on Financing for Development, sponsored by the United Nations and held in Monterrey, Mexico. So far, there has been some progress, particularly from some European donors and Japan. But even among donors who have agreed to untie aid, little has been done to make the new policy clear and known in advance for specific projects. And one of the largest donors, the United States, has done little to comply with the OECD recommendations.[3] Without more flexibility and transparency in aid decisions, it is difficult to see how relationships and aid effectiveness can be significantly improved. Getting rid of tied aid is really a litmus test for donor willingness to change the aid relationship. It remains to be seen if the recommendations of the Monterrey Conference—known as the Monterrey Consensus—will be fully implemented. More speeches and more conferences, with little concrete action, won't help.

*Donor-NGO Relationships*   The second difficult area is donor agency relationships with NGOs. Transparency cannot mean being all things to all people. Aid agencies cannot continue to meet with all individuals and NGOs that want to see them. As we talked about earlier, this is increasingly eating up scarce donor time and resources. More importantly, when these meetings take place without the concerned government, these contacts tend to undermine government accountability and donor transparency rather than reinforcing them. Public debate and scrutiny are essential for a successful development program. Openness needs to be incorporated into the process without the relationship between donors and NGOs or between donors and the private sector being primary. This openness must be led by the government, whether the NGOs or the entrepreneurs are indigenous or international. If this change is to take place—and it's a big change—it will have to be adequately explained so that donors are not subject to new accusations of hiding behind closed doors. Donors cannot continue to act as proxies—sometimes anointed, sometimes not—for governments.

*Unbundling Governance*   The final recommendation about transparency is also difficult to implement. Transparency is certainly a two-way street, and donor efforts to improve transparency will have little effect if they are not accompanied by government efforts to become more transparent. Donor efforts to improve their own transparency can have a positive impact on governments and possibly create a snowball effect. On the other hand, donor efforts to coerce more transparency through conditionality are unlikely to be positive. In addition, lumping together transparency issues with the more political aspects of the governance agenda has generally made governments even less receptive to donor views on these matters. Donors should consider moving away from lumping together transparency issues—related to administrative efficiency, accountability, and corruption—with the more political aspects of governance, including the conduct of multiparty elections and treatment of opposition parties. This could lower tension and dispel some of the reluctance to discuss corruption and accountability issues, allowing for more influence and effective dialog. The comprehensive approach to the governance agenda, while intellectually attractive, has been a source of irritation to most African governments. It inevitably brings on fears about the loss of national sovereignty and excessive internal interference by donors. Even receptive governments, in reality, put up with it rather than embrace it. Separating that agenda into more manageable bits, and starting with the less politically charged elements, could revitalize the dialog and lead to concrete gains in transparency and trust.

## Open Communication

There is no question that communication among donors and governments is improving, helped in part by some of the new processes embedded in the PRSP and CDF approaches.[4] Most of the government and donor representatives I interviewed did not see this as a central issue. They felt that there were ways to get their messages across and that many conversations were frank and open. This is encouraging and needs to built upon. But how?

*More Informality*   It's actually quite easy. More informal exchanges through conversations and emails need to be encouraged. And new technologies, such as videoconferences and the Internet, can help span large distances. But both governments and donors need to be aware that informality and speed can lead to confusion. There needs to be a climate where both sides are free to question and clarify what the other party really means. And for that to happen, development communication needs to move away from the language of diplomacy. Fewer formal statements and "white papers"—and more conversations—are needed. Getting rid of diplomatic euphemisms without sacrificing good manners would be helpful. All of this would have the added benefit of bringing both donors and governments closer to the private sector. Businessmen constantly complain about long speeches, long papers, and obtuse messages they get from both development agencies and governments.

*Climate Shift*   For open communication to take place, however, a climate shift within the donor agencies is necessary. Staff in donor agencies must be able to admit they don't know everything. "Taking stabs in the dark," "seat of the pants recommendations," and asking for additional studies instead of confronting difficult issues are just not acceptable if aid relationships are to improve. At the same time, donor staff must respect government officials, the way that governments work, and their decision-making styles and procedures. This is no easy task when the procedures—or the people—are slow, inefficient, and even arbitrary. But there is simply no getting around this issue. Leaping over government procedures or circumventing them is a short-term solution that does not work. Donor agencies learned this when they tried to establish project implementation units apart from normal government structures in the 1970s and 1980s. As soon as the project funding was gone, little was left. The same thing can happen with policies. Special administrative decrees can be reversed as easily as they are promulgated, and the seesaw of policy reform begins all over again. As one minister said to me: "Even under bad governments, it's good to remember that people believe in their governments more than they believe in the people who come from outside." While one might wish this weren't true—and fortunately, it isn't true in every case—in many African countries, the statement rings true. So working with those countries' governments, in a climate of mutual respect, is essential.

*Culture and Communication*    Donor staff need to recognize how fundamental culture is to communication. In the most easily understandable form, it is difficult for open communication to exist without a shared language. Conversations—and the balance of power among the participants—change dramatically depending upon whose language is in play. If both donors and governments share a common language—for example, Great Britain and most of southern Africa—it is not an issue. But in all other cases, it *is* an issue. Sometimes with enormous good will on both sides, the difficulties can be overcome. But more frequently, language difficulties get in the way of informal communication and establishing relationships built on trust. And that applies not only to the working staff, but to senior aid officials as well. Language skills are being eroded by the lack of staff continuity in a number of donor agencies and by the use of staff who are expected to work across five or six countries involving at least two and sometimes three languages. Highly specialized technical experts who work all over the world and who make one or two brief visits to a country cannot reasonably be expected to speak that particular country's language. But most donor staff do not fall into this category. English may increasingly be the international language for business, but it is not the international language for trust.

Understanding that different cultural assumptions can underlie a conversation may be even more important, and certainly more difficult, than learning a language. One person can show concern; the other person hears paternalism. One person's informality is another person's lack of respect. The examples are endless. It is far from easy to listen to yourself using another person's perspective. But that's exactly what needs to be done if communication between donor and government officials is to improve. It is not a question of convincing the other person that your way of doing things is the right way, but rather a question of learning to recognize and accept different cultural assumptions. Once again, revealing cultural differences by learning about the other's culture and experience can definitely help. Just as donor staff have had to keep up with the times by learning new computer programs—many with different commands and different logic—they also need to keep up by learning the language of culture. And that requires some training and frequent interaction over an extended period of time—"luxuries" many donor staff just don't have.

## CORE ELEMENTS OF TRUST: SHARED PURPOSES, COMMITMENT, AND RELIABILITY

Increasing familiarity, encouraging transparency, and improving communication will help build trust and strengthen aid relationships. But despite the importance of the measures outlined in the previous section, those improvements are in some sense just window dressing; the core elements of trust must be present. Everyone must understand—donors and governments alike—that they are playing the same game while on the same team. The rules can't change during the game, and players can't miss practice, be late for the game, or drift on and off the field.

### Shared Purposes

As we saw earlier, there is some recognition that at least on a formal level, donors and African governments share the same objectives—improving the lives of African people. But as soon as one goes beyond that generalization, the picture becomes more complicated.

*Clear Objectives* The first complication is that in reality, there are multiple objectives in play. Clarifying and simplifying objectives—including getting rid of practices such as tied aid that don't necessarily contribute to development objectives—are steps already mentioned. And while it is perhaps inevitable for both donors and governments to have multiple objectives, it is prudent to remember the caution from economist Jan Tinbergen that it generally doesn't work to try and reach multiple targets with only one instrument. If multiple objectives continue at play, then it really doesn't make much sense to judge aid's ability to reduce poverty as the measure of effectiveness and results. If foreign aid is really to be used for development and poverty reduction, then the other objectives need to take a back seat. This alone would be a radical change in the aid industry.

*Agreed Priorities* The second complication is that while there may be shared overall objectives, donors and governments do not generally have the same sense of priorities for the short run or agree on concrete ways to reach those objectives. This is where the aid relationship really runs into difficulties. Fortunately, there are some solutions. Exercises to create mission statements within large corporations and development institutions have been helpful in clarifying common goals and have reinforced common values among employees. Similar exercises looking at long-term development goals, involving government officials, civil society representatives, and donors, have begun in some countries. This type of exercise can be useful in clarifying common and complementary objectives that are sufficiently strong to link all three groups. It can also lessen mistrust by making more explicit those areas where political interests or analyses lead to different conclusions among the actors.

This is really the spirit behind the recent Poverty Reduction Strategy (PRSP) exercises that attempt to establish a common path for development initiatives. It is also the spirit behind the Comprehensive Development Framework (CDF) launched by the president of the World Bank in January 1999. The CDF recognizes the complexity of development and is intended to help governments, civil society, and donors establish a common framework and a set of long-term priorities to which all parties can contribute and provide support.[5] Although less ambitious, sector-wide approaches or sector investment programs try to establish common objectives and investment priorities within a particular sector such as education, health, or agriculture. They are part of the new movement in the aid industry to work on establishing common frameworks and implementation plans for investment. The Monterrey Consensus document urged donors and aid recipients to use development frameworks "that are owned and driven by developing countries and that embody poverty reduction frameworks."[6]

*Political Courage*   While PRSPs, CDFs, and sector investment programs are steps in the right direction, these exercises will contribute nothing but stacks of paper unless there is political will to conquer the real issues behind the current morass of conflicting and overlapping objectives and programs. The first is that contravening personal motivations must be reduced. Civil service and salary reform in African countries and clear performance criteria and codes of conduct for donor staff must be a part of this picture. Second, and even more important, the political determination and will to implement the programs contained in PRSPs, CDFs and sector investment programs must exist. Common frameworks necessarily limit the autonomy of donor agencies and their ability to attend to the multiple demands put forth by a variety of groups, both in donor and African countries. While these groups must be brought into the picture, hard choices will have to be made, and not all issues and concerns will receive priority treatment. To pretend that these varied interests can all be accommodated or reconciled is just that—a pretense. There needs to be a clear understanding on the part of donor agencies that things will not necessarily be implemented according to their strong preferences, priorities, and timetables. Donors will have to move away from parochial interests and short-term deadlines. How to accomplish this, without losing support for foreign aid, is the central dilemma. Visible successes are vital for continuing support for foreign aid, but success will ultimately depend on donors, individually and collectively, becoming less visible in the process.

*Donor Coordination*   Without even going as far as PRSPs and CDFs, this dilemma shows up time and time again in aid coordination efforts. In most aid-dependent African countries, local donor representatives have groups that meet regularly, formally or informally, to coordinate aid. Similar efforts take place at the international level through such groups as the Special Program of Assistance for Africa (SPA). There are two striking features of these groups. First, many do not include formal participation by African governments. The rationale is that the donor countries "have to get their own act together" before talking to the governments. The second striking feature is that despite many years of meetings, "their act" is still not together—donor coordination is far from being achieved. Different priorities, conditions, and procedures are still prevalent among donors.

There is, perhaps, a new recognition of the problem. In February 2003, a high-level meeting was held in Rome to discuss "harmonization." The meeting recognized that the wide array of donor requirements placed heavy burdens on African and other recipient countries, and that donors' practices frequently did not fit with country priorities or budget cycles. Perhaps more importantly, it recognized that donor coordination must fundamentally be a government-led initiative.[7]

Observed through the prism of relationships, it's not surprising that coordination has been elusive. How can aid coordination be meaningful and effective without the central involvement of the government? The argument in the past has been that most African governments are not prepared or capable of taking on that responsibility, hence the World Bank and United Nations are called on to perform that role on their behalf. But if a government cannot be trusted to coordinate aid, how can one expect the resulting development programs to be successful?

*More Trust in Governments*   Moves to improve aid coordination and strengthen the governments' role have been timid. They include holding annual World Bank–led country aid coordination meetings, known as Consultative Group (CG) meetings, in the countries themselves instead of traditional European venues such as Paris. CG meetings have been held in a host of African countries over the last several years, including Tanzania, Malawi, Mozambique, and Zambia. Some of these meetings have been jointly chaired by the concerned government and the World Bank or by the government itself. In the international aid community, these meetings have been hailed publicly as great successes, but in private, opinions vary. Not surprisingly, a number of donors are less than enthusiastic about this change, claiming that holding the meeting in the country constrains their ability to frankly critique government actions. This lack of enthusiasm is shared by some African governments. Although nearly all support the change of venue for CG meetings publicly, privately they express doubts. Why? Some donors claim this is because the governments fear public exposure of their flaws. But governments say they fear the change of venue because it will make it even easier for donor priorities to overshadow government priorities.

These different perspectives show that the aid relationship, and hence aid coordination efforts, are far from being on solid ground. Declarations in Rome or merely changing the venue of CG meetings will not lead to common priorities or improved aid coordination if the preceding steps of intensive dialog and establishing trust have not taken place. The same is true of PRSPs and CDFs. As it stands today, a number of donors and governments, while formally recognizing the need for comprehensive development frameworks, view these as nothing more than World Bank or IMF attempts to "take over" the development dialog or to have those agencies' development agendas become *the* development agendas for the concerned countries. This impression becomes heightened, particularly on the governments' side, because PRSPs have become mandatory to receive balance of payments support from the World Bank and IMF and debt relief from the donors.

The intent of this mandatory link is to ensure that the money will be spent on poverty-related activities. The message to governments, however, is that they cannot be trusted to listen voluntarily to donor concerns or to spend the money wisely. Moreover, the donors themselves *all* want to be individually involved in the CDF and PRSP processes because they don't trust each other and fear that their individual interests and views will not be adequately considered.

On top of all this, there are criticisms and suspicions surrounding the whole approach of aid coordination and harmonization. Some have likened PRSPs to the central planning documents of the Soviet era, inimical to a market-based approach. Others insist that they are just new instruments designed to provide window dressing for what is already an excessive amount of control and collusion among donors. For them, there is already too much coordination among donors. The "cartel of donors," or the "cartel of good intentions" as Easterly refers to it, gangs up on governments (or else co-opts them), hides its members' failures, and collectively exercises spin control. What is needed is more competition, not less.[8]

I am sure that there are some Africans that share these views, and like most extreme views, there are valuable kernels of truth. But these criticisms take for granted an underlying climate between donors and governments that is adversarial in nature and fraught with mistrust. They are also founded on a deep suspicion of institutions and bureaucracies in general. They don't entertain the possibility that there are gains possible through collaboration among donors *and* between donors and governments. They underestimate the powerful effect that ideas and relationships can have in bringing about change.

The Rome Harmonization Forum, the Monterrey Consensus, and the Millennium Development Goals (MDGs) constitute explicit efforts to improve aid coordination—efforts that go much further than those of the past. Nonetheless, unless the overall climate of mistrust changes, all of these aid coordination efforts may yield little. The PRSP and CDF processes, coupled with the MDGs, could help enhance opportunities for dialog and forge common visions and programs. But it is hard to see how these can work if, as in the case of PRSPs, they basically become conditions for receiving money and become tied to deadlines for debt relief and other types of financial support.

### Commitment and Reliability

That brings us to commitment and reliability. Conditionality cannot be used as a proxy for commitment. Countries need to be judged not on their promises and willingness to agree to stringent and frequently impossible conditions, but on their actions. Those actions need to be evaluated within a specific context and not against some abstract standard that may not even be attainable in donor countries. And if countries are carrying out reform programs, they need dependable support. Donor reliability is central to a healthy aid relationship. Avoiding uncertainty is a deep-rooted cultural value in African societies. Reliability becomes even more important than it is in most donor countries where a certain amount of change and uncertainty is tolerated, if not welcomed, and where the roots of a government's political support run much deeper.[9]

The problem today is that the conditions set for aid are generally independent of a longer-term, more comprehensive vision and do not recognize that there are multiple paths to achieve the same objectives. Genuine engagement in PRSP processes and a focus on reaching MDG targets could change this situation, but in the meanwhile, conditions remain relatively short-sighted, focused on means rather than results, and take the place of a more arduous process of dialog and mutual influence. Donors cling to their own vision and the stubborn belief that leverage will induce change, and that commitment and action can somehow be induced. The relatively poor record on compliance with this type of conditionality speaks for itself. Even when the leverage works and there is short-term compliance, the evidence is undeniable that it does not work in the long run. Where conditionality has worked or seemed to work, commitment was *already* there.

*Ending "Stop-Go" Aid*   Moreover, there are circumstances where the use of leverage has been counterproductive. When deadlines and conditions are not met and aid continues to flow, the whole credibility of the aid process is severely undermined. That's generally what happened in the 1980s. In reaction, in the 1990s donors became more tough-minded about compliance. In a number of countries, this has led to a "stop-go" process of aid, with frequent aid suspensions and delays. When that has happened, the relationship between government and donors has sharply deteriorated, and really put a stop to productive dialog and donor ability to influence policies. With a government that is struggling with reform and beset with internal conflicts, the stop-go pattern of aid weakens the will of reformers and strengthens the hand of those most cynical about aid and the role of donors. Aid—and the donors—become the problem rather than the solution. Donors cannot simply put conditions on the table and walk away.

*A Different Vision for Development*   Unfortunately, there are no easy answers. Donors cannot, will not, and should not simply give money away. Some form of commitment to common objectives and goals must exist. But real commitment and common, mutually agreed objectives and goals will only emerge through an arduous and lengthy process of thinking and struggling together. There really is no substitute for aid relationships that have developed over time, where governments and their civil societies sit with donors and discuss what really matters. There has to be a different way of working together. Both sides must engage in a different dynamic—be flexible, ignore momentary tensions, and keep talking.

Working together also implies changes in the way that aid decisions are made. The political will to isolate aid decisions from short-term pressures is essential. The public—as well as some NGO and donor agency staff—must come to realize that aid is not a quick fix, and that constructing a building or a road is not development. Furthermore, the donors—and NGOs—would need to understand that what *they* see as priorities are not necessarily those of the *country*, or at least that they cannot be easily implemented immediately given the cultural, economic, and social reality of a particular country. Impressions formed on the basis of scant knowledge of a country's history and even less knowledge about the cultural context must stop influencing the decision-making process. Donors need to refrain from looking in a mirror and then telling African governments that this is what development is all about.

Developing a different vision and building the related relationships and frameworks require a long-term commitment. Those involved need to either live in the countries or make continuous and frequent visits over a period of years. This not only applies to donor staff, but also to NGOs, whether local or international. Similar to the challenge faced by donors, NGOs must build relationships with governments, rather than putting the bulk of their efforts into lobbying donor agencies.

The trend toward merging diplomatic and development worlds in Africa also needs to be rethought. Painstaking dialog over an extended period of time and a process of mutual influence based on concrete discussions of development alternatives are perhaps not best handled by diplomats. While diplomats understand the value of dialog, their principal task is to represent their country's interests. Their orientation is more toward current events and short-term concerns. Moreover, many do not have the requisite training to understand the complexities of development. While diplomats have an important role, it is very different from the role—and vision—needed on the development front.

*Multiyear Financing*   Just as governments need to back up their words
with actions, donors must do so as well. Donors need to demonstrate that they
are not "fair weather friends" and show their commitment to a country over
the longer term. This means that donors must be prepared to enter into more
flexible, longer-term, multiyear financial commitments and scrupulously live
up to their commitments.[10] Under these arrangements, donors would also be
protected from the short-term pressures of various groups. Sudden donor re-
versals of policy, such as George Bush's decision to cut off aid for family planning in developing countries as soon as he entered office, would cease.

Do multiyear financial commitments mean that money will continue to
flow even when there are short-term obstacles and delays? Does this bring
with it a risk that some funds will be wasted and put in the hands of governments that will squander the funds and reverse course? Undeniably this will
happen. Given the sudden changes of policy that beset many African governments on a regular basis, sometimes it will be difficult to tell if there is a temporary stumbling or a more lasting change. But at least the longer timeframe
will give a government the chance to right itself, and over time, it will limit
donor losses and make aid more effective. If a government fails to live up to
agreed longer-term objectives—and even more importantly—withdraws
from the continuing dialog, the donors have a clear course of action. Until
agreed objectives are met and a new dialog is reestablished over a period of
time (measured in years, not weeks), there would no new multiyear (or other)
commitments. The highly disruptive stop-go pattern of aid would cease. If aid
goes on, it goes on for an extended period of time. If aid stops, it stops for an
extended period of time. The crisis atmosphere surrounding aid in most
struggling countries would cease. The key tests would be quality of the dialog
and the continuing trend toward fulfilling multiyear objectives and reaching
MDGs, rather than today's practice of taking snapshots and making snap
judgments.

Some governments will not be able to live up to this type of arrangement.
Without the ever-looming threat of financial crisis and what amounts to constant nagging by the donors, they will falter and fail. But those are precisely the
governments where over time, little that is permanent is being achieved any-
way, and aid is not effective. For those governments, the consequences of their
actions will be serious—and lasting over an extended period of time—enough
time for a government and its citizens to look at the results and understand

the consequences of pursuing different objectives. And for those governments that are struggling *and* genuinely committed to improving the lives of their citizens, this change in the modality of aid—and in the aid relationship—will be welcome. It will also provide the needed breathing space to consolidate gains and make further, and possibly even faster, progress over the years. And that breathing space will allow trust and mutual influence to grow, and encourage "uncertain reformers" to become "committed reformers."

Multiyear financing would end the current practice of temporary stars or "aid darlings" and create more stable relationships. It admittedly carries with it some challenges and risks. What happens to those governments that fail? September 11 and the plight of Afghanistan clearly point to the risk of abandoning countries and pushing them to become "international outlaws." In those cases, dialog, to the extent possible, and technical and educational contacts and exchanges should continue, as well some humanitarian assistance if feasible.[11] But this would mean a much lower financial commitment and should not be confused with development financing per se. It bears repeating that it is illusory to think that large amounts of aid can induce a change in government policies or reduce poverty in those situations.

And what happens if new governments come into power and demonstrate an early commitment to dialog and reform, but have no track record? In those cases, a special financing arrangement could be worked out for an interim period of one to two years, with a clear understanding that a multiyear financing arrangement would follow automatically if the dialog deepens, progress is in the right direction, and agreement is reached on longer-term objectives and goals. This interim arrangement would only be available to new governments (not new finance ministers or governments experiencing sudden "changes of heart") with clearly stated reform objectives and a commitment to serious dialog with donors.

*Less Donor Competition*   Lengthening the timeframe for aid and basing it on agreed objectives and goals would do a lot to bolster perceptions of donor commitment and reliability within African countries. Along with this, and quite possibly as the centerpiece of reform, competition among donors simply must cease. Donor efforts today are fragmented, creating costly duplicate efforts while at the same time leaving large gaps. Moreover, time spent with various donors and their separate programs is overtaxing governments and robbing them of time needed for more careful consideration of priorities, including internal discussion and debate within government and with civil society. It is telling that most African ministers of finance spend more time in Europe and the United States than they do visiting rural areas of their country.

The donor community, over the last few years, has recognized this problem. In some countries, sector investment programs, PRSPs, and CDFs are being used to try and coordinate all development efforts, including those of the donors. Alongside these efforts, a number of donors have begun work on harmonizing disbursement, procurement, and monitoring procedures in order to lower the administrative costs to governments. Some have already begun to move more of their financing away from project-specific interventions toward more general budget support. All of these efforts are recognized and encouraged in the Monterrey Consensus document and the Rome Declaration on Harmonization.[12] If these efforts take root, both the reliability and transparency of donor efforts will improve. Nonetheless, this is not a simple process. In some cases, separate procedures result from the need to provide tied aid benefiting donor country companies and consultants. In the multilateral development agencies, specific procedures are in place to ensure that there is fair competition among member countries for contracts and strict accountability for the funds provided. The latter is especially important since some member governments, like the United States, have explicitly stated that future support for these agencies will depend on their ability to show concrete results with the funds provided. So, what is a good idea in principle is difficult in practice. As long as donors insist on separate programs and individual "accountability" for their aid efforts, the problems and transaction costs of aid coordination will continue to undermine aid relationships and effectiveness.

*Common Pool of Donor Funds*    So donors claim they need separate, visible programs in order to "sell" aid in their respective countries. Wouldn't lower costs to provide aid and an increase in aid effectiveness be the best selling point for aid? A common donor pool of funds—based on intensive and permanent dialog and agreed objectives and goals—would solve, in one stroke, many of the problems and costs associated with the tangled web of donor coordination that exists today.[13] Common pooling arrangements would mean that individual donor financing for projects and programs would cease. All development-related aid would be deposited in a central account for use by the government in its overall program. That program would be one that has been intensely discussed both internally and with donors. It would be based on agreed objectives and expected results, but the donors would not be involved in the day-to-day arrangements for spending the money, except possibly in some circumstances as invited advisers.

Many argue that this is where the donor community is headed, albeit slowly, because individual countries are not yet able to properly manage and efficiently spend large pools of money without a great deal of donor assistance and management support. But that brings us back to the question of trust. In today's world there is insufficient dialog and more rules than relationships. Multiyear financial commitments, and even more so, a common pool of donor funding, appear to be foolhardy. That may be partly true. As it stands today, donor agencies are a bundle of contradictions, agreeing on the one hand that long-term objectives and government-owned programs are key, while on the other hand continuing to make project by project decisions on aid and maintaining large portfolios of specific projects. Making these changes has major bureaucratic implications and entails risks to both aid levels and institutional survival that most aid agencies are not ready to face. But it is also true that unless you trust someone and give them the responsibility to make decisions and mistakes rather than doing it for them, chances are they will never learn. And it's difficult to hold someone accountable for results—and repayment—unless they are fully responsible for spending. All the talk and efforts surrounding African capacity-building seem hollow unless they are accompanied by real shifts in decision making and control.

And there would be safeguards. Just as in the case of multiyear financial commitments, under common pooling arrangements, if governments decide to terminate the dialog or substantially deviate from the objectives, the common pooling arrangement would terminate, and aid would be withdrawn at the end of the agreed period. And it would take serious effort—and time—to restart the dialog and eventually the aid. The costs to governments of going in a different direction would be high, if not prohibitive. The risks to donors, in reality, would not be much higher than those that exist today.

### A Sea Change for the Aid Business

The above recommendations imply a radical shift in the way aid decisions are made and development agencies go about their business. A good deal of the problem in going from rhetoric to reality is *not* the agreement on general principles, but the major changes that would have to take place in the processes and institutions that today form the backbone of the aid industry.

*Aid Budgets*   The external pressures on aid agencies need to be lightened. In the first instance this means that short-term planning horizons, the feeling that less is more, and the present practices of scrimping, false savings, and cutting corners all have to go. Along with these, pressure to lend or provide certain amounts of aid annually also must go. Administrative budgets and aid amounts need to be determined by performance judged on a multiyear basis rather than by historical trends or what a country received the previous year.

These recommendations may seem utopian—and expensive. But if the donor community were prepared to create a new climate for aid, including multiyear financial frameworks, it is likely the cost of providing aid would be lower. Money could be redirected from painstaking project planning and micromanaging activities. Instead, donors would work with governments and their civil societies to forge comprehensive long-term visions, define key medium- and long-term objectives, and maintain a continuous dialog. Today, some aid agencies are trying to do both—with insufficient funds—and not doing a very good job on either.

*Staffing Changes*   Redirecting aid efforts to focus on development frameworks rather than projects has serious implications for aid agencies. Initially, the savings would not be great. Over the medium term, substantial savings are likely, but much more importantly, there would be increased dialog, trust, and aid effectiveness. This kind of redirection is not easy; it implies a different breed of staff. In the first instance, a cultural shift among staff is needed to work toward more dialog, teamwork, and cooperation—both internally and externally. And as the shift took root, the type of expertise among core donor staff would have to change from specialized, project-focused technical skills to broader analytical and people-oriented skills, including a greater understanding of cultural influences and an ability to integrate specific policies and investments into a broader framework. While donors could continue to provide concrete project advice on demand, this would not be a routine or obligatory feature of their aid. This would lead to much smaller groups of in-house technical specialists supported by a pool of known consultants. Those consultants, ideally after an initial contact sponsored by the aid agency, would go on to establish independent relationships with the governments and work directly for them. With some of the better consultants, this is already happening on an ad hoc basis.

In addition, the bureaucratic and psychological burdens on aid agency staff need to be lightened. One element of lifting those burdens is for aid agencies to recognize that their staffs are doing a difficult, and at times dangerous, job, and to show that their efforts are appreciated. It's less a question of big perks and privileges and more a question of recognition, but it's also a question of having the right staff in the right place. If the aid climate in Africa is to change, the staff working on Africa must have a commitment to excellence, but excellence does not mean staff who can write the most polished reports or are the world's foremost technical experts who zip from country to country. Undoubtedly, there's room and a need for some of those. But excellence working in the African context really means staff who are able to blend technical expertise with political, institutional, social, cultural, and environmental knowledge. They must have open minds and hearts—an ability to see another's perspective and to blend it with their own. For that to happen staff cannot be inexperienced, continuously changing, or working on four or five countries at once. Unfortunately, the legacy of the aid effort in Africa has created a distinct set of difficulties and prejudices related to working on Africa. If aid agencies are really serious about changing the relationship and improving aid effectiveness, the leadership will need to establish some short-term programs and incentives that bring their best and most experienced staff into the effort. Those staff must be committed to stay for several years, with an emphasis on developing relationships instead of reports and legal agreements.

*Rebuilding Morale*    Staff morale in at least some of the aid agencies must be rebuilt. If internal trust is missing, it is unlikely that staff will have the necessary support and attitudes to work on building trust with their counterparts in the African governments. A large part of the morale problem is linked to the overall climate for aid, so improvements in that climate will also help staff morale. But there's also a great deal of work to be done internally. Staff cannot continue to bear the brunt of external pressures, whether reflected in fluctuating budgets, constant shifts in priorities, new initiatives without funding, elaborate bureaucratic procedures adopted for the sake of better public relations, or endless meetings with interested parties who should really be addressing their concerns to the governments and citizens of African nations. Each agency needs to have a detailed diagnosis of the principal sources of stress and pressures upon staff and to painstakingly design a mitigation program. Those programs must recognize the inherent contradiction that is today at the heart of a great deal of the stress. Staff feel responsible and are held accountable for programs whose ultimate success or failure lies outside their grasp. Yet, giving up whatever control they do have is a difficult decision, both individually and institutionally. Nonetheless, the shift of responsibility must be toward African governments so that both the credit and the blame—as well as the day to day work—lie squarely there. As it stands now, there is no clear ownership of failure. Far worse, there's no clear ownership of success.

*Improve Communication and Coordination*   Communication and coordination within each donor need to improve. There are real differences in perceptions between staff located in capitals far away from Africa and those living in the country. And there are also different viewpoints among the institutions involved within a particular donor country. When those perceptions and viewpoints translate into different positions and attitudes that are communicated to a particular African country, the resulting confusion undermines reliability and trust. Just as there is a need for painstaking dialog between donors and African governments, so too is there a need for internal dialog within each donor.

Forging a common long-term vision, together with the government, civil society, and other donors, along with multiyear commitments, would go a long way toward solving this issue. But even now there is much that can be done to improve vertical and horizontal communication and ensure that all involved staff understand what is going on and a donor's official position on specific issues. Too often, the time and effort to do this is ignored because it's largely invisible to the outside world, except when the communication breakdown results in embarrassment. Improving internal donor communication and coordination is more about "being good" than "looking good."

*Measuring Success*   One of the greatest difficulties in instituting change has been that neither the aid industry nor governments have the right tools and perspectives to measure success. The frantic, but futile search for short-term measurements of success clouds careful monitoring of trends and progress toward agreed objectives. The fascination with numbers, an inevitability in an industry led by economists, coupled with a fixation on the short-term, an inevitability in a process involving politicians, leads to measuring the wrong things, mainly inputs. In today's anxiety for most aid agencies to look good, massive bureaucratic number-crunching exercises place enormous burdens on staff with little real payoff. What's more, they can be counterproductive, leading to policy flip-flops and decisions based solely on short-term perspectives.

An ongoing dialog and methodology to monitor progress and overall trends is needed to improve the effectiveness of aid, one that focuses on improved living conditions for the citizens of African countries. In principle, national development frameworks and the Millennium Development Goals provide the right kind of framework, but there's still a lot of work to be done to adapt these to specific country contexts and to define the methodologies and techniques for measuring progress along the way. And measurement needs to consider that development is a long-term learning process involving both qualitative and quantitative changes. The difficulties of finding and using adequate measures should not be underestimated. As Senge says: "When we act in a complex system the consequences of our actions are neither immediate nor unambiguous. . . . This leads to the 'dilemma of learning from experience.' . . . We learn best from experience, but we never experience the consequences of our most important decisions."[14] That is certainly true of the development process that goes on through generations. And this creates real contradictions for the aid industry. The spirit of the results-based aid approach coming into vogue is the correct one. But there is a danger, in today's environment, that too much attention and effort will be focused on measuring short-term results and indicators, particularly if aid budgets are strictly tied to getting results. The slow process of development in Africa is out of sync with today's world of fast food, electronic opinion polls, and instant computer messaging.

*Barriers to Reform*    Besides being able to measure success, the barriers to reform are formidable. Despite the many calls for reform—and even some emerging consensus over the direction it needs to take—there are few actors who are willing and able to sell real change in the donor countries. Aid agencies, those who know most about development, are ill-placed to be the champions of radical reform, since radical reform will bring major disruption to their agencies and greatly reduce the extent of their control—and their budgets. NGOs, particularly the strong international ones, similarly would have to completely redirect their efforts from lobbying parliaments and aid agencies—nice comfortable jobs—to jumping into the fray at the country level and actually confronting the many difficulties and challenges. Other arms of government, such as the diplomatic corps, departments and ministries of commerce, and treasuries and finance ministries, are against this approach because it would rob them of their perceived leverage to influence those items that are front and center on their agenda—usually short-term matters not necessarily linked to economic development. And while African governments certainly would support this approach, the history of aid in Africa makes them less than credible supporters in the eyes of most public policymakers in the donor countries.

But if somehow sufficient and credible champions could be found to educate the public and clearly demonstrate the need for different aid arrangements and relationships, it could really change the picture. Aid relationships would move away from intense dependency, mutual finger pointing and mistrust, and fuzzy accountabilities and results. There would be greater government autonomy, clear responsibilities and accountabilities, and reasonable timeframes to achieve and evaluate results. The relationship would be founded on trust. In cases where donors have to walk away, it would be much clearer to all that despite the needs, there's no use in providing additional aid at this time. Some may argue that the withdrawal of aid in those circumstances would create further chaos on a continent already fraught with strife. But the risks of continuing to do business as usual—with limited, tangible results—are even greater. The gradual, but unmistakable, crumbling of countries like Zimbabwe, and the on-off aid programs in countries like Kenya, clearly show the limitations of the current approach. It is time to move the aid agencies away from being unreliable taskmasters, and in some cases convenient scapegoats, to reliable and trusted partners. And where the aid agencies and the government cannot be trusted partners, aid should not be part of the scene.

Where does all of this leave us? As both a participant in and observer of the aid process, I am left with an uncomfortable feeling. At present, aid and the aid relationship in Africa are still fraught with difficulties. At the same time, as I have tried to point out in this chapter and elsewhere in the book, there is a process of change underway. Concerns over aid effectiveness are leading to changes and reforms—some quite promising. And there is a growing recognition that the relationship between donors and African governments needs to change.

It is tempting to conclude by saying that there are two paths to reform. There is the slow route that the industry is currently pursuing in fits and starts. That route means moving slowly toward CDFs in some countries, bolstering the PRSP process, convincing donors one by one to end the practice of tied aid, and putting more efforts into donor coordination and staff training, as well as pursuing some internal changes within donor agencies. And then there is the fast route that involves radical change and reeducating the public about aid in Africa. It implies redefining the roles of donors and NGOs and moving the industry rapidly out of projects and programs and into multiyear financial arrangements with country pools of donor funds to be used by governments in pursuit of agreed objectives and outcomes. Accompanying this would be rapid "cultural revolutions" within the aid agencies themselves.

I can hear many of my colleagues saying that there is no basic disagreement over how aid to Africa needs to evolve, but it's all a question of timing and realism. And they may be right. It may be unrealistic to expect anything other than a slow evolution in terms of solving problems and building trust in the relationship. But the trouble with piecemeal reforms is that they don't create a groundswell of change and each reform takes place in relative isolation. Synergies are lost. While one or two bricks may fall from the wall, the wall remains. Piecemeal reform is like attacking the wall with a chisel when a bulldozer is needed. And a little tinkering here and there doesn't stop people in their tracks and shake them up. It is not enough to convince people that the wall is really coming down and with it, the vicious cycle of lack of trust, poor results, and continued aid dependency. People living near the wall—both on the donor side and government side—simply don't believe that big changes are possible. That cynicism is crippling.

It is tempting to say that Africa's leaders should take the lead and tear down the wall. And they need to do so, but they cannot do it alone. They must be given the room to act and a reason to believe that their cynicism is misplaced. That simply cannot happen in today's world where all too frequently deadlines take the place of dialog, political correctness dictates that the "right development path" is one that closely imitates the European and American experience, and governments, along with their civil societies, do not have the room to try and fail and try again and succeed. Too often, when donors speak of government-led efforts, they mean governments traveling the path that the donors have chosen, and at the donors' pace.

This is not simply an issue of giving governments the money and walking away. There is plenty of valuable experience worldwide that needs to brought to bear on the problems of Africa. But it is only in an atmosphere of trust and mutual influence that that experience can be successfully meshed with the cultural traditions and actual conditions within Africa today. There may be other ways to do this than moving rapidly to a scenario of intensive, ongoing dialog, accompanied by multiyear financial commitments and pooled donor funds, but it needs to be done. To its credit, the donor community is increasingly focusing on the right kinds of issues in its debates on aid. The question is whether action will rapidly follow. Real dialog, real thinking together, real change, and real results still lie ahead.

Given the subject of this book, it's fitting to close with the words offered by senior African government officials when asked what advice they would give to donors in order to improve aid relationships and aid effectiveness.

"Give time for us to do the program. Be financiers, not doers."

"More trust. More dialog."

"Privilege the dialog. Don't give up too soon."

"Listen a little bit . . . you will be more influential if you have success in dovetailing your interests with the interests of the country."

And finally,

"Listen more to the governments. And believe a little more."

## NOTES

1. As quoted in a *Washington Post* editorial, "There is No Wall," March 12, 2002. See also Wolfensohn 2003.

2. "The Politics of Compassion: Aid as an Industry," *The Washington Post*, January 26, 2001, p. A19.

3. See the OECD website www.OECD.org and de Jonquiyres 2003.

4. IDA and IMF 2002 and World Bank 2003.

5. For a more detailed explanation of the rationale and coverage of the CDF, see Wolfensohn 1999.

6. United Nations 2002, para .43.

7. High-Level Forum on Harmonization 2003.

8. Easterly 2002.

9. For an analysis of the political difficulties of economic reform in Africa, see Herbst 1998.

10. The idea of multiyear aid commitments is not new. See, for example Herbst 1998.

11. Along these lines, in January 2004, the World Bank created a new trust fund to aid the most needy countries in capacity-building and urgent needs.

12. United Nations 2002, para. 43, and High-Level Forum 2003.

13. The idea of a common pooling arrangement is not new. See Riddell 1999 and Kanbur and Sandler 1999.

14. Senge 1994, p. 313.

# References and Further Reading

Abugre, Charles. 1999. "Partners, Collaborators or Patron-Clients: Defining Relationships in the Aid Industry." ISODEC: Ghana. Background document prepared for CIDA/Canadian Partnership Branch, August.

Arndt, Channing. 2000. "Technical Assistance." In *Foreign Aid and Development: Lessons Learnt and Directions for the Future*, edited by Finn Tarp. London and New York: Routledge.

Asante, Molefi Kete, and William B. Gudykunst, eds. 1989. *Handbook of International and Intercultural Communication*. Newbury Park, Calif.: Sage.

Bearak, Barry. 2003. "Why People Still Starve." *The New York Times Magazine*, July 13.

Berg, Elliot. 1993. *Rethinking Technical Cooperation: Reforms for Capacity Building in Africa*. New York: United Nations Development Program.

Biggs, Stephen, Don Messerschmidt, and Barun Gurung. 2003. "Contending Cultures Amongst Development Actors." Draft paper for the Workshop "Order and Disjuncture: The Organisation of Aid and Development" at the School of Oriental and African Studies, University of London, September 26–27.

Burnside, Craig, and David Dollar. 1997. *Aid, Policies and Growth*. Washington D.C.: World Bank Working Paper No. 1777.

Bush, George W. 2002. Speech to the Inter-American Development Bank. Washington, D.C., March 14.

Carlsson, Jerker, Gloria Somolekae, and Nicolas van de Walle, eds. 1997. *Foreign Aid in Africa: Learning from Country Experiences.* Uppsala, Sweden: Nordiska Afrikainstitutet.

Carlsson, Jerker. 1997. "The Effectiveness of the Aid Relationship in Zambia." In *Foreign Aid in Africa: Learning from Country Experiences,* edited by Jerker Carlsson, Gloria Somolekae, and Nicolas van de Walle. Uppsala, Sweden: Nordiska Afrikainstitutet.

Cassidy, John. 2002. "Helping Hands." *The New Yorker,* March 31.

Clarke, Clifford C., and G. Douglas Lipp. 1998. "Conflict Resolution for Contrasting Cultures." *Training and Development* 52 (2): 20.

Coleman, James S. 1998. "Social Capital in the Creation of Human Capital." *American Journal of Sociology* 94: 95–120.

Collier, Paul. 1997. "The Failure of Conditionality." In *Perspectives on Aid and Development,* edited by Catherine Gwin and Joan M. Nelson. Washington, D.C.: Overseas Development Council.

Collier, Paul, and David Dollar. 1999. *Aid Allocation and Poverty Reduction.* Washington, D.C.: World Bank Working Paper 2041.

de Jonquiyres, Guy. 2003. "Donors Praised for 'Untying' Aid Projects." *The Financial Times,* April 23.

Deverajan, Shantayanan, David Dollar, and Torgny Holmgren, eds. 2001. *Aid and Reform in Africa: Lessons from Ten Case Studies.* Washington, D.C.: The World Bank.

Easterly, William. 2002. *The Cartel of Good Intentions: Bureaucracy versus Markets in Foreign Aid.* Washington, D.C.: Center for Global Development Working Paper No. 4.

Easterly, William, Ross Levine, and David Roodman. 2003. *New Data, New Doubts: Revisiting "Aid, Policies, and Growth."* Washington, D.C.: Center for Global Development Working Paper No. 26.

Ellis, Richard J., and Michael Thompson, eds. 1997. *Culture Matters: Essays in Honor of Aaron Wildavsky.* Boulder, Colo.: Westview Press.

Etounga-Manguelle, Daniel. 2000. "Does Africa Need a Cultural Adjustment Program?" Pp. 65–77 in *Culture Matters,* edited by Lawrence E. Harrison and Samuel P. Huntington. New York: Basic Books.

Eyben, Rosalind, with Rosario Leon. 2003. "Who Owns the Gift? Donor-Recipient Relations and the National Elections in Bolivia." Draft paper for the Workshop "Order and Disjuncture: The Organisation of Aid and Development" at the School of Oriental and African Studies, University of London, September 26–27.

Fisher, Roger, William Ury, and Bruce Patton. 1991. *Getting to Yes: Negotiating Agreement Without Giving In,* 2nd ed. New York: Penguin.

Friedman, Thomas L. 1999. *The Lexus and the Olive Tree.* New York: Farrar, Straus and Giroux.

Fukuyama, Francis. 1996. *Trust: The Social Virtues and the Creation of Prosperity.* New York: Free Press.

Gancel, Charles, and Chilina Hills. 1997. "Managing the Pitfalls and Challenges of Intercultural Communication." *Communication World* 15 (1): 24.

Gardner, Howard. 1995. *Leading Minds.* New York: Basic Books.

Gladwell, Malcolm. 2000. *The Tipping Point: How Little Things Can Make a Big Difference.* Boston: Little, Brown and Company.

Glazer, Nathan. 2000. "Disaggregating Culture." In *Culture Matters,* edited by Lawrence E. Harrison and Samuel P. Huntington. New York: Basic Books.

Gudykunst, William B., and Stella Ting-Toomey. 1988. *Culture and Interpersonal Communication.* Newbury Park, Calif.: Sage.

Gudykunst, William B., and Tsukasa Nishida. 1989. "Theoretical Perspectives for Studying Intercultural Communication." Pp. 17–46 in *Handbook of International and Intercultural Communication,* edited by Molefi Kete Asante and William B. Gudykunst. Newbury Park, Calif.: Sage.

Gwin, Catherine, and Joan M. Nelson, eds. 1997. *Perspectives on Aid and Development.* Policy Essay 22. Washington, D.C.: Overseas Development Council published by Johns Hopkins University Press.

Hall, Edward T. 1977. *Beyond Culture.* Garden City, N.Y.: Anchor Books.

———. 1983. *The Dance of Life: The Other Dimension of Time.* New York: Doubleday.

———. 1991. "Context and Meaning." Pp. 46–55 in *Intercultural Communication: A Reader,* edited by Larry A. Samovar and Richard Porter. Belmont, Calif.: Wadsworth.

Harrison, Lawrence E., and Samuel P. Huntington, eds. 2000. *Culture Matters.* New York: Basic Books.

Herbst, Jeffrey. 1998. "The Structural Adjustment of Politics in Africa." Pp. 431–49 in *Africa: Dilemmas of Development and Change,* edited by Peter Lewis. Boulder, Colo.: Westview Press.

High-Level Forum on Harmonization. 2003. *Rome Declaration on Harminization.* Rome, Italy, February 25.

Hofstede, Geert. 1980. *Culture's Consequences: International Differences in Work-Related Values.* Beverly Hills, Calif.: Sage.

Holman, Michael. 2004. "Africa's Potemkin Deception Is Fooling the World." *The Financial Times,* January 20, p. 21.

Hopkins, Raul, Andrew Powell, Amlan Roy, and Christopher L. Gilbert. 1997. "The World Bank and Conditionality." *Journal of International Development* 9 (4): 507–16.

Inglehart, Ronald. 1997. *Modernization and Postmodernization: Cultural, Economic, and Political Change in Forty-Three Societies.* Princeton, N.J.: Princeton University Press.

Inglehart, Ronald. 2000. "Culture and Democracy." Pp. 80–97 in *Culture Matters,* edited by Lawrence E. Harrison and Samuel P. Huntington. New York: Basic Books.

Inglehart, Ronald, and Wayne Baker. 2000. "Modernization, Cultural Change, and the Persistence of Traditional Values." *American Sociological Review* 65 (February): 19–51.

International Development Association and International Monetary Fund. 2002. *Review of the Poverty Reduction Strategy Paper (PRSP) Approach: Main Findings,* Washington, D.C., March 15.

Kanbur, Ravi. 2000. "Aid, Conditionality, and Debt in Africa." Pp. 409–22 in *Foreign Aid and Development: Lessons Learnt and Directions for the Future,* edited by Finn Tarp. New York: Routledge.

Kanbur, Ravi, and Todd Sandler with Kevin M. Morrison. 1999. *The Future of Development Assistance: Common Pools and International Public Goods.* Policy Essay No. 25. Washington, D.C.: Overseas Development Council published by Johns Hopkins University Press, September.

Killick, Tony. 1997. "Principals, Agents and the Failings of Conditionality." *Journal of International Development* 9 (4): 483–95.

Klitgaard, Robert. 1997. "Applying Cultural Theories to Practical Problems." Pp. 191–202 in *Culture Matters: Essays in Honor of Aaron Wildavsky,* edited by Richard J. Ellis and Michael Thompson. Boulder, Colo.: Westview Press.

Lancaster, Carol. 1999. *Aid to Africa: So Much to Do, So Little Done.* Chicago: The University of Chicago Press.

Lewis, Peter. 1998. *Africa: Dilemmas of Development and Change.* Boulder, Colo.: Westview Press.

Lindblom, Charles E., and David K. Cohen. 1979. *Usable Knowledge: Social Science and Social Problem Solving.* New Haven, Conn.: Yale University Press.

Mazrui, Ali A. 1999. "Globalization and Cross-Cultural Values: The Politics of Identity and Judgement." *Arab Studies Quarterly* 21 (i3): 97.

Milburn, Trudy. 1997. "Bridging Cultural Gaps." *Management Review* 96 (1): 26.

Mosle, Sara. 2000. "The Vanity of Volunteerism." *New York Times Magazine,* July 2.

Mosley, Paul, Jane Harrigan, and John Toye. 1991. *Aid and Power: The World Bank and Policy-Based Lending,* 2 vols. New York: Routledge.

Neilson, Brett. 1997. "Institution, Time-Lag, Globality." *Journal of Communication Inquiry* 21 (2): 23.

Neuliep, James W., and Daniel J. Ryan. 1998. "The Influence of Intercultural Communication Apprehension and Socio-Communicative Orientation on Uncertainty Reduction During Initial Cross-Cultural Interaction." *Communication Quarterly* 46 (1): 88.

Ngulube, Naboth. 1997. *Culture and Development.* Lusaka: n.p.

North, Douglass C. 1990. *Institutions, Institutional Change and Economic Performance.* Cambridge: Cambridge University Press.

Obasanjo, Olusegun. 1987. "Africa: The Year 2000 and Beyond." Third Economic Commision for Africa Silver Jubilee Lecture. Addis Adaba: United Nations.

Picciotto, Robert. 1998. "The Logic of Partnership: A Development Perspective." Washington, D.C.: World Bank.

Putnam, Robert D. 2000. *Bowling Alone: The Collapse and Revival of American Community.* New York: Simon and Schuster.

Riddell, Roger C. 1999. "The End of Foreign Aid to Africa? Concerns About Donor Policies." *African Affairs* 98 (392): 309–35.

Rieff, David. 1998. "In Defense of Afro-Pessimism." *World Policy Journal* 15 (i4): 10.

Samovar, Larry A., and Richard E. Porter. 1991. *Communication Between Cultures.* Belmont, Calif.: Wadsworth.

Samovar, Larry A., and Richard E. Porter, eds. 1991. *Intercultural Communication: A Reader*. Belmont, Calif.: Wadsworth.

Schreiter, Robert. J. 1996. "Communication and Interpretation Across Cultures: Problems and Prospects." *International Review of Mission* 85 (337): 227.

Senge, Peter M. 1994. *The Fifth Discipline: The Art and Practice of the Learning Organization*. New York: Currency Doubleday.

Shweder, Richard A. 2000. "Moral Maps, 'First World' Conceits, and the New Evangelists." Pp. 158–71 in *Culture Matters*, edited by Lawrence E. Harrison and Samuel P. Huntington. New York: Basic Books.

Stein, Howard. 1998. "Japanese Aid to Africa: Patterns, Motivation, and the Role of Structural Adjustment." *Journal of Development Studies* 35 (i2): 27.

Stepanek, Joseph F. 1999. *Wringing Success from Failure in Late-Developing Countries*. Westport, Conn.: Praeger.

Tannen, Deborah. 1998. *The Argument Culture: Moving from Debate to Dialogue*. New York: Random House.

Tarp, Finn, ed. 2000. *Foreign Aid and Development: Lessons Learnt and Directions for the Future*. New York: Routledge.

Tsikata, Tsidi M. 1998. "Aid Effectiveness: A Survey of the Recent Empirical Literature." IMF Paper on Policy Analysis and Assessment. Washington, D.C.: International Monetary Fund.

United Nations. 2002. "Final Outcome of the International Conference on Financing for Development, Monterrey Consensus," English version, March 22.

United Nations Development Programme (UNDP). 2003. *Human Development Report 2003*. New York: United Nations.

Van de Walle, Nicolas. 1999. "Aid's Crisis of Legitimacy: Current Proposals and Future Prospects." *African Affairs* 98 (392): 337–52.

Van de Walle, Nicolas and Timothy A. Johnston. 1996. *Improving Aid to Africa*. Washington, D.C.: Overseas Development Council (distributed by the John Hopkins University Press).

Vasquez, Ian. 2003. *The New Approach to Foreign Aid: Is the Enthusiasm Warranted?* Washington D.C.: Cato Institute Foreign Policy Briefing No. 79.

Walzer, Michael. 1997. *On Toleration*. New Haven, Conn.: Yale University Press.

Weisner, Thomas S. 2000. "Culture, Childhood, and Progress in Sub-Saharan Africa." Pp. 141–57 in *Culture Matters*, edited by Lawrence E. Harrison and Samuel P. Huntington. New York: Basic Books.

White, Howard, and Oliver Morrissey. 1997. "Conditionality When Donor and Recipient Preferences Vary." *Journal of International Development* 9 (4): 497–505.

Wolfensohn, James. 1999. "A Proposal for a Comprehensive Development Framework, Discussion Draft." Washington, D.C.: World Bank.

Wolfensohn, James. 2003. "A New Global Balance: The Challenge of Leadership." Address to the Board of Governors of the World Bank Group at the joint Annual Discussion, Dubai, September 23.

Woodcock, Michael, and Deepa Narayan. 2000. "Social Capital: Implications for Development Theory, Research and Policy." *The World Bank Research Observer* 15 (2): 225–49.

World Bank. 1998. *Assessing Aid.* New York: Oxford University Press.

———. 1999. *The Drive to Partnership: Aid Coordination and the World Bank.* Washington D.C.: Operations Evaluation Department.

———. 2000. *Can Africa Claim the 21st Century?* Washington, D.C.: World Bank.

———. 2001a. *Poverty Reduction Strategy Paper Sourcebook.* Washington, D.C.: World Bank.

———. 2001b. *The Onchocerciasis (Riverblindness) Programs: Visionary Partnerships,* Africa Regional Findings, No. 174. Washington, D.C.: World Bank.

———. 2003. *Toward Country-led Development: A Multi-Partner Evaluation of the Comprehensive Development Framework.* Washington, D.C.: World Bank.

Zhu, Zhichang. 1999. "The Practice of Multimodal Approaches, the Challenge of Cross-Cultural Communication, and the Search for Responses." *Human Relations* 52 (i5): 579.

# Index

# About the Author

**Phyllis R. Pomerantz** began her career at the World Bank in 1979 working as a rural development specialist on Latin America and especially Brazil. Since 1989 she has held a series of managerial positions, including Chief of Brazil Agriculture (1989–1992), Chief of Infrastructure Operations in Southern Africa (1992–1994), and Country Director and Country Manager of Zambia and Mozambique (1994–2000). Following her special assignment to research and write about aid relationships in Africa, she was appointed the World Bank's first Chief Learning Officer, the position she currently holds. She is responsible for providing strategic vision and leadership for the World Bank's staff learning program.

Prior to working at the World Bank, she was an Assistant Professor of Political Science at Hartwick College (New York), a lecturer at Tufts University (Massachusetts), and a research associate at the Pontifical Catholic University of Peru. Ms. Pomerantz holds two master's degrees and a Ph.D. in international development from the Fletcher School of Law and Diplomacy. She is fluent in English, Spanish, and Portuguese.